CHOCOLATE
COOKERY

with
AARON MAREE

PHOTOGRAPHY BY ASHLEY MACKEVICIUS
STYLING BY WENDY BERECRY

BayBooks
An imprint of HarperCollins*Publishers*

ABOUT THE AUTHOR

At just 23, Aaron Maree has become one of the leading pastry chefs in Australia with numerous awards and honours to his credit. He began as a general chef's apprentice but quickly found his real interest lay in the art of pastry making. Aaron became fascinated with the artistic possibilities of chocolate.

In 1988 he won the prestigious Patissier '88 competition, his profession's highest award, competing against the finest pastry chefs in the country whilst still only an apprentice. Completing his training the same year with the Sheraton Hotel Corporation, Aaron spent the next two years travelling and working in some of the finest hotels in Europe.

He returned to Australia in 1990 to take up a position as the Brisbane Polo Club's executive pastry chef and in the same year won the Young Queenslander of the Year award in recognition of his outstanding achievements in the hospitality industry.

Author of Cakes, Tortes and Gâteaux of the World and Cookies, Biscuits and Slices of the World, he is a member of the invitation only World Master Chefs Society. He has travelled extensively to study techniques and research recipes, and has worked in major hotels in the United Kingdom and Europe, including the Relais and Chateaux Group.

In 1991 Aaron was awarded a travelling scholarship to the United States to learn more of the art of the patissier from American masters.

A BAY BOOKS PUBLICATION
An imprint of HarperCollinsPublishers

First published in Australia in 1992 by Bay Books of
CollinsAngus&Robertson Publishers Pty Limited
(ACN 009 913 517)
A division of HarperCollinsPublishers (Australia) Pty Limited
25-31 Ryde Road, Pymble NSW 2073, Australia

HarperCollinsPublishers (New Zealand) Limited
31 View Road, Glenfield, Auckland 10, New Zealand

HarperCollinsPublishers Limited
77-85 Fulham Palace Road, London W6 8JB, United Kingdom

Copyright © Bay Books 1992

This book is copyright.
Apart from any fair dealing for the purposes of private study, research, criticism or review, as permitted under the Copyright Act, no part may be reproduced by any process without written permission. Inquiries should be addressed to the publishers.

National Library of Australia Card Number and
ISBN 1 86378 006 8
Photography by Ashley Mackevicius
Styling by Wendy Berecry

Printed in Singapore

5 4 3 2 1
96 95 94 93 92

CONTENTS

INTRODUCTION

Chocolate not only delights the eye and the tastebuds, but provides me with endless opportunities to create wonderful confections and concoctions. Chocolate is unique. It tests my imagination and flair as a chef more than any other ingredient. It offers so many possibilities for moulding, modelling, topping, covering, binding, flavouring and for decoration - the ultimate finishing touch. Cooking with the chocolate products we have today is just as much an exciting adventure as the story of its discovery.

In this book, I have included some of my favourite recipes. As a chef, I always weigh and measure in grams and litres. However, for your convenience I have included the nearest cup equivalent.

This book is dedicated to all closet chocoholics. The time has come to be proud of your fetishes, cravings and insatiable taste for the finer things in life, chocolate, chocolate, chocolate ....

Company acknowledgments:
Rod Slater, Anna Permezel and James C.T. Tan, Cadbury Schweppes Pty Ltd, Vic.
John Reid, Marketing Manager, Defiance Milling, Qld
David Watson, Marketing Manager, The Good Egg Corp., NSW
Jan Liddle and Paul Lawson, Glad Products of Australia
Brian Cox, State Manager, Socomin International Fine Foods, Qld
John Dart, Trumps Nuts and Dried Fruits, Qld
Mark Villiers, Marketing Manager, Bonlac Foods Pty Ltd
Kenwood Kitchen Appliances

ALL ABOUT CHOCOLATE

The love of chocolate has a long history. For hundreds of years the cocoa tree, *Theobroma Cacao*, was cultivated by the Maya Indians, the Inca of Peru and the Aztecs of Mexico in the forests of Central and South America. Its fruit appeased the gods, was plied in trade, and prized as a pleasurable drink. The Mayans boiled their cocoa beans with maize. In ancient Mexico, chocolate was the national drink. Montezuma, it is said, preferred his chocolate flavoured with vanilla and beaten to a froth like the consistency of honey. Whereas Hemando Cortez, conqueror of Mexico in 1519, had a sweet tooth and liked to take his royal drink with sugar.

The cocoa tree is a native of the equatorial forests and flourishes in rich, deep, loose soils. For healthy growth, cocoa trees prefer an average shade temperature of around 27°C and an annual rainfall of least 1900 mm. The tree is rather like an apple tree in size and shape, growing about seven metres high. They take from about five to eight years from planting to return their first harvest and, when mature, yield two harvests a year. The small wax-like flowers and ripe pods can often be seen growing side by side.

Carefully guarding the secrets of cultivation, the Spanish first introduced cocoa trees into Trinidad then to their other colonies in the West Indies and the Philippines. Cocoa is now grown in West Africa, South America, New Guinea and Malaysia.

In the seventeenth century, drinking chocolate was introduced to the courts of Spain, Italy, Germany, France and England. Although the Spanish were unable to keep secret the method of preparation, chocolate remained an expensive luxury. When the first chocolate house was opened in London in Bishopsgate in 1657, chocolate cost from ten to fifteen shillings a pound.

In 1826, J.S. Fry and Sons advertised a chocolate lozenge - 'a pleasant and nutritious substitute for food while travelling or when unusual fasting is caused by an irregular period of mealtimes.'

The chocolate we know today, however, was not produced until the Dutch discovered how to press cocoa butter out of cocoa beans. The pressed beans could then be used to make a less fatty cocoa drink, and the cocoa butter was used to make the eating chocolate.

In Britain, Fry appears to have been the first to use this technique in producing their chocolate 'delicieux à manger' which went on sale in 1847. They were followed two years later by Cadbury.

John Cadbury, who had started in business as a tea and coffee merchant in 1824, founded the firm of Cadbury in England in 1831. He manufactured a range of 'balanced' cocoas, including a substance called 'Iceland Moss'. In 1866, the firm of Cadbury, directed by George and Richard, the sons of John, brought out 'Cocoa Essence', a pure cocoa product made possible by the Dutch invention. The firm's example was followed by J.S. Fry and Sons who produced a pure cocoa two years later.

As a result of the manufacture of pure cocoa, a large surplus of cocoa butter became available, thus making it possible for manufacturers, with Cadbury in the lead, to make eating chocolate and chocolate confectionery.

In this new development there was considerable competition from the French, who for many years had maintained a European reputation for the quality of their chocolate fruit crêmes.

The invention of milk chocolate is widely attributed to Sir Hans Sloane, the famous eighteenth century physician. Cadbury marketed a 'milk chocolate' prepared after the Sloane recipe from 1849 until 1855. This was not, however, milk chocolate as we know it.

Milk chocolate is, in all probability, a Swiss invention, and was made as early as 1876 by Daniel Peters of Veney, near Lausanne. Until the early years of the present century, Swiss milk chocolate was preferred to any other. It was not until 1904 that the Swiss monopoly was seriously challenged. In that year Cadbury introduced a new and milkier chocolate after years of experimentation and the investment of much money. This was Cadbury Dairy Milk, also known by its familiar abbreviation, 'C.D.M.'

Today, Cadbury Schweppes makes a wide range of chocolate and cocoa products for eating, drinking and cooking. The recipes in this book make full use of all these products.

The Chocoholic's Pantry

Cooking chocolate is a smooth blend of cocoa, liquor and cocoa butter which has less sugar added than 'eating' chocolate making it suitable for addition to sweet recipes. There are two types of cooking chocolate available which both have specific uses - they are pure cooking chocolate and compounded cooking chocolate, which are both available in dark, milk or white varieties.

Pure cooking chocolate is designed for recipes which require cooking as pure chocolate. It withstands high temperatures, while still giving a strong chocolate flavour. Pure chocolate is particularly suitable for baked goods such as cakes, cheesecakes, and pies and for confectionery such as fudge.

Compounded chocolate contains less cocoa solids than pure chocolate and has the addition of more stable fats, either vegetable or coconut oils. The addition of oils makes compounded chocolate easy to work with as it melts more readily and retains a high gloss when re-set. Compounded chocolate is particularly suitable for cold desserts, decorative chocolate recipes, moulding, toppings, fillings and sauces.

Varieties of Cooking Chocolate

Dark cooking chocolate (both pure and compounded) has the highest amount of cocoa liquor which gives it the strongest chocolate flavour and a very dark colour.

Milk cooking chocolate (both pure and compounded) has the addition of milk solids which makes the chocolate flavour less strong.

Milk chocolate is a popular eating variety and has many uses, particularly in recipes prepared for children when a milder chocolate flavour is required.

White cooking chocolate (both pure and compounded) is a blend of cocoa butter and milk solids, and though it is the least stable to work with, it is popular for its distinct flavour, creamy texture and its colour contrast to other chocolates. White chocolate is particularly popular for use with summer fruits.

Chocolate Shapes and Sizes

Cooking chocolate (both pure and compounded) can be purchased in a number of forms. These are:

Blocks: Blocks of cooking chocolate are very convenient for decorative uses such as for neat chocolate shavings or chocolate curls. They can easily be broken into even pieces for weighing and melting prior to cooking.

Buttons: The small uniform shape of cooking buttons makes them simple to weigh and very easy to melt. Compounded buttons become very fluid when melted, making them ideal for coating or moulding. Buttons can also be used whole for decorating purposes or novelty cakes.

Chocolate dots: Chocolate dots are very small, dark chocolate pieces, specially formulated for melting in a microwave oven. They provide a strong, pure chocolate flavour and hold their shape when used in cooked foods such as biscuits or slices. Chocolate dots come in convenient sachets designed for easy melting and mess-free piping and decorating. Also, use Chocolate dots whole for creative decorating of cakes or slices.

Cocoa: Cocoa is a powdered, pure chocolate product that has a slightly bitter flavour as it contains no added sugar. Cocoa is a convenient way to achieve a strong chocolate flavour, particularly in baked goods where no other fat or liquid is required. For best results cocoa should be sifted with other dry ingredients or blended to a paste with hot liquid. Cocoa is very good for pastries, biscuits and cakes.

Drinking Chocolate: Drinking chocolate is a mixture of cocoa and powdered sugar. Drinking chocolate is ideal for drinks, coating and icings and also gives an excellent finish when dusted or sprinkled over food such as cakes or truffles.

Cadbury has an extensive range of both Cadbury pure chocolate products and Unichoc compounded chocolate products. They are:
- Cadbury Dark Cooking Chocolate 250g
- Cadbury Milk Cooking Chocolate 250g
- Cadbury White Cooking Chocolate 250g
- Cadbury Chocolate Dots 200g
- Cadbury Bournville Cocoa 125g
- Cadbury Bournville Cocoa 250g

*Cadbury Chocolate Dots;
Cadbury Dark, Milk
and White Cooking
Chocolates; Cadbury
Drinking Chocolate and
Cadbury Bournville
Cocoa*

*Unichoc Dark and Milk
Compounded Cooking
Chocolates; Unichoc Milk
Buttons, Unichoc Dark
Cooking Compounded
Buttons and Unichoc
White Buttons*

•Cadbury Bournville Cocoa 375g

•Cadbury Drinking Chocolate 250g

•Cadbury Drinking Chocolate 500g

•Unichoc Dark Buttons 375g

•Unichoc Milk Buttons 375g

•Unichoc White Buttons 375g

•Unichoc Dark Compounded Block 300g

•Unichoc Milk Compounded Block 300g

CHOCOLATE LOVER'S KITCHEN

Cooking with chocolate requires very little special equipment. Following is the equipment I used in making these recipes.

MIXING BOWLS

Stainless steel bowls are often used, although any type of non-porous bowl will suffice when baking. Always wipe bowls before use. Although plastic bowls can be used for dry mixings, always whip egg whites in a stainless steel bowl.

CHOCOLATE EGG MOULDS

Available in most supermarkets, and specialty kitchen shops prior to Easter, it is up to the creative cook to choose the most suitable size and design. Keep moulds meticulously clean and well washed after use.

SCRAPER

Plastic cake scrapers are a shortened version of the spatula, allowing for close contact with the food at the bottom and sides of mixing bowls.

SWISS ROLL PAN

Measuring 18 cm x 28 cm x 2 cm (with slight variations), these pans are used for producing slices and, of course, for Swiss rolls. To protect pans, try not to cut baked goods in the tray as this will cut the metal and can lead to rusting and discolouration of the tin surface.

PAINT BRUSH

Small paintbrushes or pastry brushes are useful for painting small designs onto the sides of Easter eggs, for painting chocolate onto moulds or for touching up small mistakes. Several sizes are available.

COMB SCRAPER

Comb scrapers are simply plastic cake scrapers which have been cut on both sides with teeth markings, which allow for decorative designs to be scraped around the sides of cakes or for the production of two tone chocolate curls. Comb scrapers are also available in metal triangles which have three sizes of teeth.

ASSORTED PALETTE KNIVES

Palette knives have a long flexible stainless steel blade with a rounded end, usually mounted onto a short wooden handle. They are used for flattening cake mixtures into trays, removing products from trays and for icing cakes. Sizes range from 10 cm to 40 cm in length and can be in straight form or bent just below the handle to give height.

GRATER

Flat, round or square, graters are perfect for grating chocolate into shavings and fine curls, and for grating rind from citrus fruits.

MUFFIN PAN

Available in 6, 12 and 18 hole pans, these pans can also be bought according to size of muffin required and range from 4 to 5 cm to 9 to 10 cm in diameter. Muffin pans can be used for any small cakes as well as for patty cakes. If cakes need leavering from their mould then use a blunt object or palette knife to avoid the risk of cutting the metal.

PIPING BAG AND NOZZLES

When purchasing piping bags, always buy bags that are joined without stitching as mixtures can leak from this seam. Ideally buy a plastic piping bag which has been melted at the seam or glued. Do not buy fabric piping bags as these can absorb flavours and tend to perish quickly.

Always clean piping bags in warm water with a little detergent and rinse well before standing in a well ventilated area to dry. Never store piping bags wet as they will deteriorate.

Piping nozzles can be bought in either plastic or metallic form and in a number of sizes, though usually in only two shapes, plain or star.

DARIOLE MOULDS

Dariole moulds are small, steep-sided, cylindrical containers, usually made from aluminium. Shapes tend to vary giving quite a choice to the cook with flair. Most moulds will fit 250 to 300 ml of mixture and these moulds can be used for baking, refrigerating, steaming or boiling. If these moulds are not available then use tea or coffee cups, but do not use the heirloom china.

5 Beat the egg whites until stiff peaks form and then gently fold through the egg yolk mixture.

6 Pour three-quarters of the mixture into the prepared pan and bake for 40 minutes.

7 When baked the cake should have shrunk slightly from the sides of the pan. Allow it to cool in the pan and it should sink in the middle as it cools.

8 When completely cool, remove the sides of the pan from the cake and pour the reserved quarter of the mixture into the hollow on top of the cake. Take a little of the mixture and spread it thinly around the sides of the cake, spreading the remainder evenly over the top.

9 Place the cake onto a plate or serving dish and then begin arranging the chocolate squares around the sides, making certain that each one overlaps the others. Cut remaining squares into triangles with a hot knife and then press these triangles into the top of the cake.

10 Refrigerate cake for 1 hour, then remove and dust with cocoa powder before cutting with a hot knife to serve.

SERVES 12

✤ **HOT CHOCOLATE FUDGE**

For a delicious hot chocolate sauce, try Hot Chocolate Fudge: *Melt 60 g unsalted butter together with 120 g Cadbury Milk Cooking Chocolate, in a double boiler. Add ¼ cup (60 g) caster sugar and stir till dissolved. Add ½ cup (125 ml) cream, stir until combined.*

CHOCOLATE UPSIDE-DOWN CAKE

8 whole glacé cherries

16 canned apricot halves, drained

125 g unsalted butter

1 cup (150 g) brown sugar, lightly packed

2 x 60 g eggs

1½ cups (180 g) plain flour, sifted

3 tablespoons Cadbury Bournville Cocoa, sifted

3 tablespoons Cadbury Drinking Chocolate, sifted

1 tablespoon baking powder, sifted

½ cup (125 ml) milk

1 Preheat the oven to 180°C (350°F).

2 Lightly grease a 24 cm round springform cake pan and line with baking paper.

3 Cut each cherry in half and sit one half of the cherry in each of the 16 apricot halves. Place these face down in a pattern on the base of the lined cake pan.

4 Cream the butter and sugar until light and fluffy. Add the eggs one at a time, beating well after each addition. Add the sifted flour, cocoa, drinking chocolate and baking powder and when partly mixed in, add the milk and continue to mix until a smooth batter is formed.

5 Gently spread the mixture evenly over the apricot halves.

6 Bake for 35 minutes or until cake springs back when lightly touched.

7 As soon as cake is baked, turn upside down and peel away the baking paper. Serve immediately for the most compliments, otherwise brush over lightly with some boiled apricot jam, allow to cool and serve cold with a hot chocolate sauce .

SERVES 10 TO 12

TRIPLE CHOCOLATE SURPRISE

100 g unsalted butter, softened

⅔ cup (100 g) brown sugar

1 x 60 g egg

60 g Cadbury Dark Cooking Chocolate, melted

90 g sour cream

2 tablespoons (40 ml) milk

1 cup (135 g) plain flour, sifted

1 teaspoon bicarbonate soda

3 tablespoons Cadbury Bournville Cocoa

WHITE CHOCOLATE CREAM

⅔ cup (100 ml) thickened cream

2 tablespoons (30 g) icing sugar, sifted

60 g unsalted butter

200 g Cadbury White Cooking Chocolate, chopped

MILK CHOCOLATE CREAM

⅓ cup (100 ml) thickened cream

2 tablespoons (30 g) icing sugar, sifted

60 g unsalted butter

200 g Cadbury Milk Cooking Chocolate, chopped

DARK CHOCOLATE CREAM

½ cup (125 ml) thickened cream

250 g Cadbury Dark Cooking Chocolate, chopped

CHOCOLATE CURLS

150 g Unichoc White Buttons

150 g Unichoc Milk Buttons

150 g Unichoc Dark Buttons

1 Preheat the oven to 180°C (350°F).

2 Lightly grease a 19 x 19 x 7 cm square cake pan and line with baking paper.

3 Cream butter and sugar together until light and fluffy. Add the egg and combine well. (Mixture may curdle slightly, but do not worry). Add the melted chocolate to the butter mixture and beat in quickly before the chocolate sets.

4 Mix the sour cream and the milk together and add to the chocolate butter mix along with the sifted flour, bicarbonate soda and cocoa.

5 Pour the cake mixture into the prepared pan and bake for 30 to 35 minutes.

6 Allow cake to rest in the pan for 20 minutes, then turn out onto a cake wire to cool.

7 **TO MAKE WHITE AND MILK CHOCOLATE CREAMS.** Place the cream into a saucepan with the icing sugar and butter and stir slowly while bringing to the boil. Remove the boiling liquid from the heat and immediately add the chopped chocolate. Stir until the chocolate has melted and a smooth liquid is formed. Place the liquid into a bowl and refrigerate until cold.

TO MAKE DARK CHOCOLATE CREAM. Place cream in saucepan and stir slowly while bringing to the boil. Remove from heat, stir in chopped chocolate until melted and a smooth liquid is formed. Place liquid in a bowl and refrigerate until cold.

8 When cold, whip each of the chocolate creams separately until light and fluffy and of a spreadable consistency.

9 Cut the cake into three layers horizontally. Spread White Chocolate Cream evenly over bottom layer. Place the next layer of cake on top and spread evenly with the Milk Chocolate Cream, then place the final layer of cake on top of these and press the whole cake down firmly to ensure it is flat.

10 Spread the top and sides of the cake with the Dark Chocolate Cream. Refrigerate the cake until chocolate curls have been made.

11 **TO MAKE CURLS.** Pour melted chocolate onto a marble slab or a stainless steel countertop and use a palette knife to spread thinly. As the chocolate begins to set, hold a large knife at a 45 degree angle to the bench top and pull gently through the chocolate. It is essential to work quickly or the

Triple Chocolate Surprise

chocolate will harden and splinter. Curls should be 4 to 5 cm in length.

12 Starting in one corner of the cake, press a row of white chocolate curls over a 4 cm wide strip of the cake. Beside that place a strip of milk chocolate curls and then a strip

of dark chocolate curls. Repeat in this sequence until the whole cake has been covered. Refrigerate the cake for 30 minutes before serving.

SERVES 12

RASPBERRY FANTASY

CRUST

¾ cup (100 g) plain flour

100 g unsalted butter, softened

1 teaspoon cinnamon

40 g finely chopped almonds

¼ cup (40 g) brown sugar

FILLING

150 g unsalted butter, softened

⅔ cup (150 g) caster sugar

2 x 60 g eggs

100 g Cadbury White Cooking Chocolate, melted

200 g fresh raspberries

TO DECORATE

fresh raspberries

chocolate curls

1 TO MAKE CRUST. Gently combine the flour, butter and cinnamon. Add the almonds and brown sugar and mix until the a soft paste is formed.

2 Press the mixture into a lightly greased 23 cm round springform cake pan and bake at 180°C (350°F) for 10 minutes or until light golden brown. Allow to cool in the pan.

3 TO MAKE FILLING. Cream butter and sugar together until light and fluffy. Add the eggs one at a time and when combined, fold mixture through the melted chocolate.

4 Fold through the fresh raspberries and pour the mixture directly on top of the cooled base. Refrigerate for 1 hour.

5 Decorate with extra fresh raspberries and chocolate curls and serve immediately.

SERVES 12

CHOCOLATE GINGER SPONGE

120 g butter

¼ cup (60 g) caster sugar

30 g raw ginger, finely grated

5 x 60 g eggs, separated

60 g Cadbury Dark Cooking Chocolate, melted

3 tablespoons Cadbury Bournville Cocoa, sifted

1¼ cups (150 g) self-raising flour, sifted

¼ cup (60 g) caster sugar, extra

1½ tablespoons dark rum

icing sugar for dusting

1 Preheat the oven to 180°C (350°F).

2 Grease and line the base of a 20 cm round springform cake pan with baking paper.

3 Cream the butter and sugar with the finely grated raw ginger until light and fluffy. Add the egg yolks one at a time, mixing well between additions.

4 Add the melted chocolate to the butter mixture, mixing quickly to ensure the chocolate is combined before it hardens, then add the sifted cocoa and flour to the butter mixture and combine well.

5 Whisk the egg whites until frothy and stiff peaks begin to form. While still mixing, slowly begin adding the extra sugar. When all sugar has been added, continue to mix until it has dissolved. Fold the rum and the egg whites carefully and completely through the chocolate mixture.

6 Pour the mixture into the prepared cake pan and bake for 35 to 40 minutes or until a skewer inserted into the top of the cake comes out clean.

7 When baked allow to cool in the pan Remove and dust lightly with icing sugar and serve warm and fresh.

SERVES 8 TO 10

Raspberry Fantasy

SLICE OF HEAVEN

BASE
250 g unsalted butter, melted

150 g Cadbury Dark Cooking Chocolate, melted

4 x 60 g eggs

2½ cups (500 g) caster sugar

1¼ cups (150 g) plain flour

TOPPING
250 g unsalted butter

2 cups (360 g) icing sugar

100 g Cadbury Dark Cooking Chocolate, melted

100 g Pascall marshmallows, chopped

100 g Cadbury Chocolate Dots

100 g macadamia nuts

1 Preheat the oven to 160°C (325°F).

2 Grease a 25 x 30 x 3 cm baking pan, and line with baking paper.

3 TO MAKE BASE. Mix the melted butter with the chocolate and whisk in the eggs until smooth. Add the sugar and flour and stir again till smooth. Spread the mixture into the prepated pan. Bake for 45 minutes or until cooked.

4 TO MAKE TOPPING. While the base is baking, mix the butter and icing sugar together until light and fluffy. Add the melted chocolate to the butter mix and then fold through the chopped marshmallows, chocolate dots and nuts.

5 Once baked, allow the slice to cool slightly, however, while still warm, spread the topping evenly over the base. Refrigerate for 24 hours. Cut slice into portions using a hot knife.

MAKES 30 PIECES (APPROXIMATELY)

Slice of Heaven

BLACK FOREST FLAKE

BASE
5 x 60 g eggs, separated
½ cup (120 g) caster sugar
250 g Cadbury Milk Cooking Chocolate, melted
100 ml brandy
200 g ground almonds
1¼ cups (150 g) self-raising flour, sifted

FILLING
4 cups (1 litre) thickened cream
⅓ cup (90 g) caster sugar
425 g can sour black cherries, drained and pitted
½ cup (125 ml) kirsch or cherry liqueur

DECORATION
3 x Cadbury Flake Bars
12 red glacé cherries

1 Preheat the oven to 180°C (350°F).

2 Grease a 24 cm round springform cake pan and line the base with baking paper.

3 **TO MAKE BASE.** Beat the egg yolks and half the sugar until thick and almost white. Very gently fold the melted chocolate, brandy, ground almonds and flour into the egg yolk mixture.

4 Beat the egg whites until very stiff and then slowly add the remaining half of the sugar, mixing until the sugar has dissolved. Very carefully fold the egg whites into the chocolate mixture.

5 Pour into the prepared pan and bake 40 to 45 minutes or until the top springs back when lightly touched. Cool in the pan on a wire rack.

6 When completely cool, turn the cake out. Using a sharp serrated knife cut the cake horizontally into four even layers.

7 **TO MAKE FILLING.** Whisk the cream and the sugar until stiff. Reserve a quarter of the whipped cream in a separate bowl for final decorating.

8 Place one of the cake layers onto a plate or serving platter, cover with some of the cherries and sprinkle on a little of the kirsch. Spread with a third of the cream and then place the next layer of cake on top. Repeat this process until all of the cake layers have been used.

9 When the last cake layer has been placed on top, spread the top and sides of the whole cake with the reserved amount of whipped cream.

10 Crumble the Cadbury Flake Bars into pieces, then press the crumbled chocolate around the sides and over the top of the whole cake. Press the cherries lightly into the top of the cake at regular intervals to show portion sizes. Refrigerate for 30 minutes before serving.

SERVES 12

WICKED WONDERS

W icked Wonders are the ultimate in dinner party desserts and treats to serve anytime you fancy. Only small portions should be served or total addiction could set in.

The Step-by-Step Technique in this chapter shows how chocolate is used in moulding, for the *Bag of Fruit* and for *Chocolate Baskets*.

Bag of Fruit

STEP-BY-STEP TECHNIQUES

Carefully paint five sides of a foil-covered box with chocolate, making sure corners are well coated. Refrigerate and paint two more times.

When set, carefully slide box from the chocolate and foil. Then remove the foil from the chocolate with tweezers.

To make chocolate baskets: spread chocolate into a circular shape over a piece of plastic (cut from a freezer bag). Drape over a cup or mould.

When the chocolate has set, peel off the plastic, and fill basket with fruit or sweets.

A BAG OF FRUIT

150 g Unichoc Dark Chocolate Buttons per bag, melted

1 Carefully and neatly wrap a small packet or box approximately 10 x 6 x 3 cm with foil. Cover all but one end of the box.

2 Carefully paint all five sides with chocolate, ensuring corners are well coated. Refrigerate and repeat painting process twice

3 When finally set, carefully slide box from chocolate and foil and remove the foil from the chocolate with tweezers. Lay the finished bag on its side on a plate and fill with an array of fresh fruits.

MAKES 1

WHITE CHOCOLATE MARQUISE

2 teaspoons powdered gelatine

1½ tablespoons water

1½ tablespoons liquid glucose

3 x 60 g egg yolks

250 g Cadbury White Cooking Chocolate, melted

1⅔ cups (400 ml) thickened cream, softly whipped

24 Savoiardi Biscuits (sponge fingers)

fresh orange segments, pips removed, to serve

1 Soak the gelatine in the water in a saucepan, then place the glucose on top and melt by placing the saucepan over a gentle heat.

2 Whisk the egg yolks into the heated gelatine/glucose mixture and add the melted white chocolate.

3 Pour the white chocolate mixture into the softly whipped cream, stirring quickly to blend both mixes. This makes the marquise mixture.

4 Stand Savoiardi Biscuits or sponge fingers around the sides of a 20 cm round springform cake pan. Cover the base of the pan with any remaining biscuits.

5 Pour the marquise mixture into the prepared pan, tapping gently to ensure it flows into all holes. Allow the marquise to set for 1 hour before serving with fresh orange segments.

SERVES 12

CHOCOLATE RASPBERRY LUSCIOUS

6 x 60 g egg yolks

½ cup (100 g) icing sugar

250 g unsalted butter, softened

5 tablespoons Cadbury Bournville Cocoa

150 g Cadbury Dark Cooking Chocolate, melted

1¼ cups (300 ml) thickened cream

½ cup (100 g) icing sugar, extra

200 g fresh raspberries

1 Whisk the egg yolks and icing sugar until thick, light and fluffy. Whip the butter and cocoa together until light and fluffy and very soft.

2 Whisk the chocolate into the egg yolk mixture and then add the butter mixture and combine thoroughly.

3 Lightly whip cream with extra icing sugar.

5 Add the cream to the mixture and just before all is folded in add the raspberries and carefully combine.

6 Pour the mixture into eight fluted glasses and chill for 1 hour.

SERVES 8

Bag of Fruit

CHOCOLATE PUDDING WITH A MELTING MIDDLE

For this dessert you need 8 x 250 ml Dariole moulds

200 g unsalted butter, softened

1 cup (210 g) caster sugar

210 g Cadbury Dark Cooking Chocolate, melted

6 x 60 g eggs, separated

1½ cups (180 g) plain flour, sifted

180 g ground almonds

8 to 10 squares of Cadbury Dark Cooking Chocolate

1 Cream butter and sugar until light and fluffy.

2 Add the melted chocolate to the creamed butter mixture and mix together until combined. Scrape down the sides of the bowl to ensure all chocolate has been mixed thoroughly.

3 Add the egg yolks one at a time and combine well, then add the sifted flour and ground almonds and mix thoroughly.

4 Whisk the egg whites until frothy and stiff peaks form in a separate bowl. Carefully fold the whisked egg whites right through the chocolate mixture. Place mixture into an airtight container and set in refrigerator for 1 hour.

5 Lightly brush 8 x 250 ml Dariole moulds with melted butter and coat the base and sides of each mould with sugar.

5 Preheat the oven to 180°C (350°F).

6 Using a small spoon or spatula spread each mould with the chilled mixture, approximately 1 cm deep from the base and around the sides, and leave a small hole in the centre of the mould for a square of chocolate. Cover the chocolate and seal the mould with more of the chilled mixture. Place the moulds onto a tray and bake for 30 minutes.

7 When baked, carefully run a knife around the sides of the moulds easing each baked pudding from its container. Unmould the puddings directly onto a plate and serve with mountains of your favourite chocolate sauce.

SERVES 8

STRAWBERRY CHOCOLATE SHORTCAKES

4½ tablespoons Cadbury Bournville Cocoa

1 tablespoon instant coffee granules

1¼ cups (150 g) plain flour

⅓ cup (90 g) caster sugar

1½ teaspoons baking powder

½ teaspoon bicarbonate soda

100 g unsalted butter

½ cup (125 ml) thickened cream

200 g Unichoc White Buttons, melted

200 g cut, clean strawberries

1 Preheat the oven to 200°C (400°F).

2 Sift all dry ingredients. Add the butter and rub through the dry ingredients until mixture resembles fresh breadcrumbs. Add the cream and combine well.

3 Drop tablespoonfuls of mixture onto lined baking trays. Bake for 8 to 10 minutes or until cooked.

4 Allow to cool on a wire cooling rack and then drizzle melted white chocolate over the top of each and allow to set before serving.

5 Cut each shortcake in half and fill with cut strawberries. Serve with fresh whipped cream.

MAKES 6 TO 8

✥ **DARIOLE MOULDS**

Dariole moulds are small, steep-sided cylindrical containers, available at homeware stores. If they are unavailable, use tea or coffee cups.

Strawberry Chocolate Shortcakes

❖ ROSE PETALS

Rose petals should be separated from stems and stamens and washed carefully before use.

WHITE CHOCOLATE ROSE PETAL MOUSSE

2 teaspoons gelatine

1½ tablespoons water

1½ tablespoons liquid glucose

2 x 60 g egg yolks

250 g Cadbury White Cooking Chocolate, melted

2½ cups (625 ml) cream, very lightly whipped

rind (zest) and juice of 1 lemon

petals of 3 medium roses, different colours, washed

RASPBERRY SAUCE

200 g fresh raspberries

sugar to sweeten

2½ tablespoons cold water

1 Soak the gelatine in the water. Gently heat glucose and gelatine until melted.

2 Add egg yolks to gelatine mixture.

3 Stir in melted chocolate. Add warm mixture immediately to cream, then add lemon juice and zest and rose petals.

4 Pour the mixture into a baking pan 25 x 30 x 3 cm lined with cling film and refrigerate until firm.

5 Cut the firm mousse into 5 cm squares and serve 2 squares per serve on a raspberry sauce.

6 TO MAKE RASPBERRY SAUCE. Place hulled and washed raspberries and water into a blender with enough sugar to sweeten. Purée until smooth.

MAKES 8 TO 10 PORTIONS

BAKED CHOCOLATE CHEESECAKE

BASE

200 g shortbread biscuit crumbs

1½ tablspoons (30 g) caster sugar

3 tablespoons Cadbury Bournville Cocoa

60 g unsalted butter, melted

FILLING

650 g cream cheese

1¼ cups (240 g) caster sugar

250 g Cadbury Dark Cooking Chocolate, melted

90 g Cadbury White Cooking Chocolate, melted

2 x 60 g eggs

2 tablespoons thickened cream

⅓ cup (90 ml) sour cream

3 tablespoons instant coffee granules, mixed with 2 tablespoons hot water

1 Preheat the oven to 160°C (325°F).

2 Lightly grease a 23 cm round springform cake pan and line the base with baking paper.

3 **TO MAKE BASE.** Place the biscuit crumbs, sugar and cocoa into a bowl. Pour over the melted butter and stir until all ingredients are combined. Spread mixture over the base of the pan and press down firmly with the back of a spoon.

4 **TO MAKE FILLING.** Whip the cream cheese with the sugar until smooth and lump free. Add the melted chocolates and continue whipping so that no lumps of chocolate form.

5 Add the eggs one at a time and mix well between each addition. When both eggs are combined, scrape down the sides of the bowl. Add the cream, sour cream and instant coffee and mix until all is combined.

6 Pour the mixture over the base and place in the oven.

7 Bake for 55 minutes. Remove from the oven and allow to cool for 30 minutes. Refrigerate to completely set. Cut with a hot damp knife.

SERVES 24

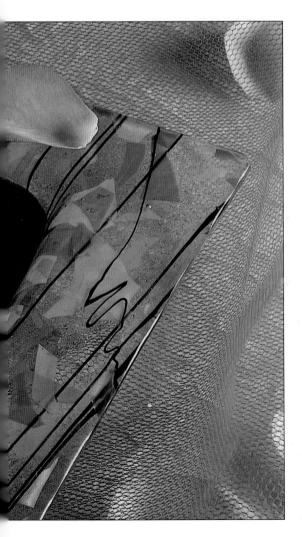

*White Chocolate
Rose Petal Mousse*

THE ULTIMATE TOLLHOUSE SLICE

BASE

⅔ cup (100 g) plain flour

1½ tablespoons Cadbury Bournville Cocoa

¼ cup (45 g) icing sugar

60 g unsalted butter

1 x 60 g egg white

TOPPING

400 g can sweetened condensed milk

1¼ cups (60 g) shredded coconut

60 g slivered almonds

100 g Unichoc White Buttons

100 g Cadbury Chocolate Dots

1 Preheat the oven to 160°C (320 °F).

2 Grease a 18 x 28 x 2 cm baking pan and line it with baking paper.

3 TO MAKE BASE. Place the flour, cocoa and sugar in a bowl and lightly rub the butter into the dry ingredients until mixture resembles fine breadcrumbs.

4 Add egg white, mix thoroughly. Turn dough onto a lightly floured surface and knead lightly. Press mixture into the prepared pan. Bake for 10 minutes until golden brown and remove from oven.

5 Reduce oven temperature to 140°C (275°F).

6 When base is cool, spread over half of the condensed milk, sprinkle with the coconut, almonds, white buttons and chocolate dots and then pour the other half of the condensed milk over the top.

7 Bake for 30 more minutes, then remove and allow to cool for 20 minutes and refrigerate for 1 hour before cutting into portions.

MAKES 24 PORTIONS

CHOCOLATE PEARLS ON A CURACAO SAUCE

3 x 60 g egg whites

½ cup (100 g) icing sugar, sifted

¼ cup (30 g) plain flour, sifted

1½ teaspoons Cadbury Bournville Cocoa

40 g unsalted butter, melted

Creamy Chocolate Mousse (see page 26) for 6 portions

110 g Cadbury Dark Cooking Chocolate, melted

1¼ cups (300 ml) Blue Curacao Liqueur

1 tablespoon arrowroot

6 Unichoc White Buttons

1 Preheat the oven to 180°C (350°F).

2 Mix the egg whites with the icing sugar until well blended. Add the flour and cocoa and lightly whisk until a smooth paste is formed. Allow batter to rest for 15 minutes. Stir in the melted butter and mix in well.

3 Place tablespoon amounts of the batter onto a lightly greased baking tray and spread each into a 5 to 8 cm circle.

4 Bake for 5 to 8 minutes, then immediately remove the tuilles (biscuits) from the tray by sliding a sharp flat knife or spatula underneath each one. Each biscuit must be immediately pressed into a round container so that they will harden into semicircular shapes.

5 When the biscuits are cold and hard lightly brush the insides of each with melted chocolate and allow to set.

6 Fill half of the tuille shells with the Creamy Chocolate Mousse.

7 Pipe a little melted chocolate onto a dessert plate and set the mousse-filled shell on top and hold until it sits firm. Place an unfilled shell slightly behind the filled shell so that it looks like a slightly open lid. (A little melted chocolate may be required to hold this in place). Place a white button on top of the mousse to resemble a pearl.

✣ **BLUE SAUCE**
*For an alternative to
Blue Curacao Liqueur,
boil 1 cup (200 g) caster
sugar and 1¼ cups (300
ml) water together for 5
minutes, then colour with
blue food colouring.*

8 Place half the curacao into a saucepan and bring slowly to the boil. Mix the other half of the liqueur with the arrowroot and stir into the boiling liquid. Continue to boil while stirring for a further minute. Remove from heat, and cool in the refrigerator.

9 With a little melted chocolate, pipe a freehand line around the pearl shells to completely enclose them. Pour the cold sauce inside this line and then serve.

SERVES 6

DEATH BY CHOCOLATE

The ultimate 'way to go'. Serve these cakes to guests without offering them a slice and watch them simply 'drool'. Each cake is a masterpiece in its own right and would suit any formal occasion or dinner party.

The Step-by-Step Technique in this chapter is for the *Chocolate Hungarian Torte* and shows the use of chocolate with collars and curls as a decoration.

Chocolate Hungarian Torte

STEP-BY-STEP TECHNIQUES

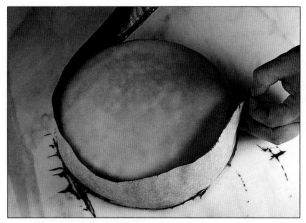

To make Collar: Spread melted chocolate on a piece of parchment paper, which is about 1 cm higher than the cake is deep, and long enough to wrap round the cake. Wrap around cake. When set, remove paper.

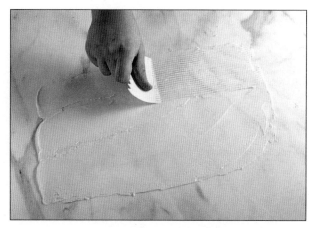

To make two-tone Curls: Spread white chocolate thinly on a marble slab or stainless steel bench top. Make ridges with a comb.

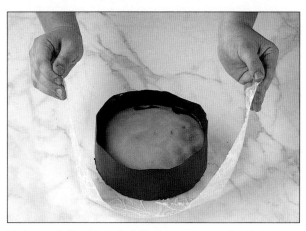

To decorate Collar: Pipe melted chocolate onto a strip of parchment paper, (same size as collar) and place paper round collar. Put in the fridge to set.

Pour melted dark chocolate over the hardened white chocolate.

When chocolate has set, remove paper carefully.

Pull a knife gently through the chocolate to form curls. Put the smallest curls on cake first, then largest and neatest curls, for the best effect.

CHOCOLATE HUNGARIAN TORTE

5 x 60 g eggs, separated

⅓ cup (100 g) caster sugar

420 g Cadbury Dark Cooking Chocolate, melted

⅓ cup (90 ml) milk

1¼ cups (150 g) plain flour, sifted

200 g ground almonds

¼ cup (60 g) caster sugar, extra

DECORATION

2 tablespoons apricot jam

200 g marzipan or almond paste

250 g Unichoc Dark Buttons, melted (for chocolate collar)

250 g Unichoc White Buttons, melted (for collar drizzle)

250 g Unichoc Dark Buttons, melted (for curls)

250 g Unichoc White Buttons, melted (for curls)

1 Preheat the oven to 150°C (300°F).

2 Grease a 20 cm springform cake pan and line the base with baking paper.

3 Beat the egg yolks with sugar until thick and pale. Very gently fold in the chocolate by hand, then the milk, flour and almonds.

4 Beat the egg whites until very stiff and frothy and slowly blend in the extra sugar, then beat until the sugar has dissolved. Very gently fold in the chocolate mixture by hand.

5 Pour the mixture into the prepared pan and bake for 30 to 40 minutes or until the top of the cake springs back when lightly touched. Cool in the pan on a wire rack.

6 When completely cold, turn the cake out of the pan and remove the baking paper from the base. Thinly spread the top and sides of the cake with the apricot jam.

7 On a lightly floured bench, roll out the marzipan into a circle large enough to cover the top and sides of the cake. Place the marzipan over the cake and mould to fit neatly. Trim the excess marzipan.

8 TO MAKE CHOCOLATE COLLAR.
Cut a strip of parchment paper which is long enough to wrap round the cake and 1 cm higher than the cake. Spread melted dark chocolate onto the paper. Wrap collar around the cake. Allow cake to stand 5 minutes in the refrigerator or until collar is firm. Remove paper from hard collar. Decorate collar with white drizzle, as instructed in Step-by-Step.

9 Make the chocolate curls and place them inside the recess of the collar and cake.

10 Mark portions with a hot knife into the collar of the cake. Then cut straight through the curls to the already marked portion cuts in the collar.

SERVES 12

Chocolate Hungarian Torte

Pyramid of Dreams

PYRAMID OF DREAMS

6 x 60 g eggs

⅔ cup (150 g) caster sugar

1 cup (120 g) plain flour, sifted

3 tablespoons Cadbury Bournville Cocoa

CHOCOLATE FILLING

1 cup (250 ml) thickened cream

2½ tablespoons orange liqueur or orange juice

500 g Cadbury White Cooking chocolate, chopped

½ cup (125 ml) orange liqueur, or orange juice (extra)

Cadbury Drinking Chocolate for dusting

1 Preheat the oven to 180°C (350°F).

2 Lightly grease three 28 x 18 cm baking pans and line each with baking paper.

3 Whisk the eggs and sugar with an electric mixer on the highest setting, or until the mixture is very thick and frothy. Lightly sprinkle the flour and cocoa over the mixture and very gently fold in by hand.

4 Pour mixture evenly between the 3 pans and using a spatula or palette knife evenly spread the mixture to the edges of each pan.

5 Bake each pan of mixture for 15 to 20 minutes or until sponge has shrunk slightly from the sides. Cool for 5 minutes before turning out onto wire racks to cool.

6 TO MAKE FILLING. Place the cream and orange liqueur into a saucepan and bring to the boil. Remove from the heat and add the chopped white chocolate. Stir until the chocolate has melted. Pour the mix into a dish and chill in the refrigerator, stirring occasionally. Do not allow the filling to become too thick; it must remain of spreading consistency.

7 Cut the edges off each sponge sheet along the longest edge, then cut each sheet in half again along the longest length. Sprinkle each strip with the extra orange liqueur.

8 Spread each strip thinly with the chocolate filling mixture and stack on top of each other, leaving the top strip plain. Chill the stack for 30 minutes.

9 Place the chilled cake lengthwise on the edge of a bench top. Place a ruler along the top edge of the cake furthest from you and cut diagonally through the bottom edge nearest you with a clean knife. The ruler and bench top are used to guide the knife. When cut, you will have 2 triangles of cake.

10 Stand the triangles so that the layers of cake run vertically. Join the 2 triangles together with a thin layer of the chocolate mixture to make a pyramid shape. Cover the sloping sides with the chocolate mixture and chill for 30 minutes. Dust lightly with drinking chocolate before serving.

SERVES 12

DEATH BY CHOCOLATE

400 g unsalted butter

400 g Cadbury Dark Cooking Chocolate

8 x 60 g eggs

1 cup (200 g) caster sugar

TOPPING

2 tablespoons warm water

300 g Cadbury Dark Cooking Chocolate, chopped

90 g unsalted butter

1 Preheat the oven to 120°C (250°F).

2 Line a 23 cm round springform cake pan with one piece of aluminium foil. Make sure no cake mix will escape.

3 Melt the butter and chocolate in the top of a double boiler, stirring occasionally so that they combine together.

4 Place the eggs and sugar into a mixing bowl and mix only to break up the eggs. Do not aerate. Add the melted chocolate mixture and stir thoroughly to combine.

5 Pour the mixture into the foil-lined cake tin and bake for 1½ hours in the preheated oven. Mixture will still seem soft and will not spring back when lightly touched. Baked cake will also seem moist internally if a skewer is inserted into it.

6 Allow the baked cake to cool for 20 minutes. Press down the crust firmly into the rest of the cake before placing it into the freezer (still in the pan) to chill for 24 hours.

7 TO MAKE TOPPING. Heat and stir water, chocolate and butter in the top of a double boiler until they melt and the mixture has a smooth consistency. Cool slightly.

8 Remove the chilled cake from the freezer and turn upside down onto a plate. Remove the foil wrapping and pour the chocolate topping over the top of the cake. Quickly spread the mixture evenly over the top and sides and then place the cake into the freezer.

9 Serve portions directly from the freezer

SERVES 16

SINNER'S SLICE

3 cups (360 g) plain flour

2½ teaspoons baking powder

3 level teaspoons bicarbonate soda

½ cup (60 g) Cadbury Bournville Cocoa

120 g unsalted butter

1½ cups (250 g) soft brown sugar

2 x 60 g eggs

125 g Cadbury Dark Cooking Chocolate, melted

1 cup (250 ml) milk

1 teaspoon vanilla essence

TOPPING

½ cup (125 ml) thickened cream

2½ tablespoons Grand Marnier liqueur or orange juice

360 g Cadbury Dark Cooking Chocolate, chopped

1 Preheat the oven to 180°C (350°F).

2 Grease a 25 x 30 x 3 cm baking pan and line with baking paper.

3 Sift the flour, baking powder, bicarbonate soda and cocoa powder twice.

4 Beat the butter and sugar until light in colour (3 to 5 minutes), then add the eggs one at a time, beating well after each addition. Add the melted chocolate to the butter mixture and beat in well.

5 Add the sifted ingredients, alternately with the milk and vanilla essence, mixing by hand. Pour into the prepared pan and bake for 35 to 40 minutes or until firm to the touch. Cool in the pan.

6 TO MAKE TOPPING. Place the cream and Grand Marnier into a saucepan and bring to the boil. Add the chopped chocolate and mix to a smooth liquid. Refrigerate the mixture, stirring occasionally until it is quite firm.

7 Place the topping into a mixing bowl and whip until very light and fluffy. Spread the topping over the cooled slice and refrigerate for 2 hours before cutting into portions.

MAKES 24 PORTIONS

✥ DEATH BY CHOCOLATE

The texture of this cake will change as the cake warms to room temperature. Keep it chilled and covered at all times for the best flavour

CHOCOLATE PAVLOVA

4 x 60 g egg whites

⅓ cup (50 g) icing sugar, sifted

1 cup (200 g) caster sugar

1 teaspoon white vinegar

3 tablespoons cornflour

3 tablespoons Cadbury Bournville Cocoa

pinch salt

TO DECORATE

1¼ cups (300 ml) cream, freshly whipped

fresh fruits

1 Preheat the oven to 90°C (175°F).

2 Line a baking sheet with aluminium foil and lightly dust with cornflour.

3 Whisk the egg whites with an electric mixer until they are stiff and frothy. Mix the sifted icing sugar with the caster sugar and slowly blend this mixture into the whisked egg whites until the sugar has completely dissolved. Fold through the vinegar and cornflour, then fold in the cocoa and salt.

4 Spread the mixture into a 20 cm circle on the tray, place in the oven and bake for 2 hours.

5 Turn the oven off and allow the pavlova to remain in the oven.

6 When both oven and pavlova are cold, top the pavlova with freshly whipped cream and fresh fruits of your choice.

SERVES 8 TO 10

⚜ CRÈME CHANTILLY

To make Crème Chantilly, a cream that stands up tall, beat 1¼ cups (300 ml) cream (well chilled) with ⅔ cup (100 g) icing sugar (sifted) and 1 teaspoon vanilla essence. Beat until stiff peaks form. Cover pavlova with the cream and top with a selection of exotic fruits.

TRUFFLE TORTE

BASE

100 g unsalted butter

⅓ cup (100 g) caster sugar

2 x 60 g eggs

1¾ cups (225 g) plain flour

4½ tablespoons Cadbury Bournville Cocoa

1 tablespoon baking powder

FILLING

⅓ cup (100 ml) milk

⅓ cup (100 ml) thickened cream

500 g Cadbury Milk Cooking Chocolate, chopped

200 g unsalted butter, softened

1½ cups (380 g) caster sugar

¾ cup (150 ml) water

4 egg whites

Cadbury Bournville Cocoa for dusting

1 Preheat oven to 180°C (350°F).

2 Lightly grease a 24 cm round springform cake pan.

3 TO MAKE BASE. Cream the butter and sugar until light and fluffy. Add the eggs one at a time and mix well. Add sifted flour, cocoa powder and baking powder and mix again until well combined.

4 Press the mixture into the prepared cake pan and ensure that it is even. Bake in the preheated oven for 35 to 40 minutes or until a skewer inserted into the cake comes out clean. Cool in the pan when baked.

5 TO MAKE TRUFFLE FILLING. Place the milk and cream in a saucepan and bring to the boil. Remove from the heat, add the chopped chocolate and stir until melted. Cool, but do not allow to set solid.

6 When the chocolate mixture has cooled, place into a mixing bowl and cream together with the butter until the mixture is light and has increased in volume.

Chocolate Pavlova

7 Place the sugar and water in a saucepan, slowly bring to the boil and boil for 7 minutes.

8 Beat the egg whites until very stiff and frothy and then slowly begin to blend in the boiled sugar syrup by drizzling it down the sides of the mixing bowl while continuing to whisk. When all syrup has been added continue whisking until cold.

9 Mix the whipped chocolate filling with the meringue mixture. Cut the baked shortcake in half horizontally and place one half on the base of the springform cake pan. Spread with three-quarters of the truffle filling and top with the other half of the cake. Press gently on the top to spread the filling evenly. Spread half of the remaining filling on top, reserving sufficient to pipe a message across the top of the torte. Chill for 2 hours before serving.

10 Unmould by running a hot knife around the sides of the pan. Place onto a serving dish and dust with Cadbury Bournville Cocoa before serving.

SERVES 12

TEMPTING TREATS

These treats can each be served as a dessert, for children's lunches or simply as an afternoon tea nibble. Keep a ready supply of them in the refrigerator for those moments when hunger strikes.

The Step-by-Step Technique in this chapter uses cocoa powder for making *Chequerboard Biscuits.*

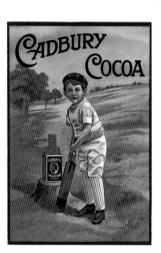

Chequerboard Biscuits

STEP-BY-STEP TECHNIQUES

Cut four 1 cm wide strips from the chocolate dough and five 1 cm strips from the white dough. Knead scrap pastry from both and roll to same length as the strips and as wide as possible.

Lightly brush dough with egg white and place white and chocolate strips alternately, brushing with egg white between layers.

After chequerboard dough has been refrigerated for 1 hour, cut into 2 mm thicknesses to bake.

CHEQUERBOARD BISCUITS

WHITE DOUGH

1¾ cups (210 g) plain flour

½ cup (90 g) icing sugar

150 g unsalted butter

1 x 60 g egg, separated

CHOCOLATE DOUGH

1½ cups (180 g) plain flour

½ cup (90 g) icing sugar

3 tablespoons Cadbury Bournville Cocoa

150 g unsalted butter

2 x 60 g egg yolks

1 TO MAKE WHITE DOUGH. Sift the flour and icing sugar together. Lightly rub the butter through the dry ingredients. Add the egg and continue mixing until a dough is formed.

2 TO MAKE CHOCOLATE DOUGH. Sift the flour, icing sugar and cocoa together. Lightly rub the butter through the dry ingredients. Add the egg yolks and continue mixing until a dough is formed.

3 Wrap each dough in plastic wrap and refrigerate for 1 hour. Then knead each dough lightly so that they are soft enough to roll. Roll both doughs into squares of equal length and width and 1 cm in thickness on a lightly floured bench.

4 Cut four 1 cm wide strips from the chocolate dough and five 1 cm strips from the white dough.

5 Knead together any scrap pastry from both doughs into a ball. Roll the scrap pastry (it should now be milk chocolate in colour) so that it is 2 to 3 mm thick, the same length as the white and chocolate strips and as wide as possible. Lightly brush the top with egg white.

6 Starting from the outer edge, place side by side one strip of white pastry, one strip of chocolate pastry and one strip of white pastry. Brush lightly with egg white. Repeat the process on top of this layer, but alternating the colours so that a chocolate strip is placed on top of a white strip and vice versa. Brush this layer with egg white.

7 Make a third layer repeating the process, again alternating the colours. Brush this layer with egg white.

8 Lightly brush egg white around the sides of the layers. Press the outer sides of the milk chocolate pastry around the chequerboard layers so that the layers are completely covered by the milk pastry. Place in the refrigerator for 1 hour.

9 Preheat the oven to 180°C (350°F).

10 Remove the chequerboard dough layers from the refrigerator and cut into 2 mm thicknesses. Place each biscuit piece onto a prepared baking tray and bake for 8 to 10 minutes, or until the white pieces are lightly browning around the edge.

11 Remove from oven and cool slightly before eating fresh.

MAKES 24

ORANGE CHOCOLATE MADELEINES

150 g unsalted butter, softened
1¼ cups (210 g) icing sugar, sifted
3 x 60 g eggs
1¼ cups (165 g) plain flour
3 tablespoons Cadbury Bournville Cocoa
1 teaspoon baking powder
1 tablespoon freshly squeezed orange juice
rind (zest) of 1 orange, finely grated
icing sugar for dusting

1 Preheat the oven to 180°C (350°F).

2 Lightly grease a madeleine tray.

3 Cream the butter and icing sugar until light and fluffy. Add the eggs one at a time and mix well after each addition.

4 Add the sifted flour, cocoa and baking powder to the mixture with the orange juice and zest. Mix until completely blended.

5 Fill the madeleine moulds three-quarters full and bake for 20 to 25 minutes or until each madeleine is springy to the touch.

6 When baked, unmould immediately and dust lightly with icing sugar before serving warm.

MAKES 24 (APPROXIMATELY)

Chequerboard Biscuits

✥ **MADELEINE TRAYS**

Madeleine trays are available with various numbers of portions. The trays consist of scallop-shaped indentations. Make sure you always buy non-stick bakeware, for the best results.

MELTING CHOCOLATE

Melt chocolate in a double boiler or a bowl placed over simmering water. first, boil water in a saucepan, then remove from heat. Break chocolate into small pieces and place in a bowl. Place bowl over saucepan and allow chocolate to melt. Never allow water to come into contact with the chocolate.

CHOCOLATE SHORTIES

250 g unsalted butter
½ cup (100 g) sifted icing sugar
1 x 45 g egg
2½ cups (300 g) plain flour, sifted
1 tablespoon Cadbury Bournville Cocoa
100 g Unichoc Milk Buttons, melted
100 g Unichoc White Buttons, melted

1 Preheat the oven to 180ºC (350ºF).
2 Cream the butter and sugar together until light and fluffy.
3 Add the egg and beat well. Add the sifted flour and cocoa powder and mix to a paste.
4 Drop tablespoons of the dough onto a lightly greased tray and bake for 10 minutes or until cooked. Cool on the tray. When cooled, drizzle with melted milk and white chocolate buttons.

MAKES 18

CHOCOLATE COCONUT BISCUITS

2 x 60 g eggs
1⅓ cups (120 g) desiccated coconut
½ cup (100 g) icing sugar, sifted
1½ tablespoons Cadbury Bournville Cocoa, sifted

1 Preheat oven to 180ºC (350ºF).
2 Lightly grease a baking tray with butter.
3 Mix all the ingredients together to form a ball and allow to rest in refrigerator for 30 minutes.
4 Place small, walnut-sized balls of mixture on the baking tray and flatten them using the back of a wetted fork, to 2 mm thick. Bake for 10 minutes.
5 When cool, remove from the tray using a flat scraper, knife or palette knife, and store in an airtight container.

MAKES 24 (APPROXIMATELY)

ROCKY ROAD SLICE

BASE
60 g unsalted butter
¾ cup (100 g) plain flour
1½ tablespoons Cadbury Bournville Cocoa
¼ cup (45 g) icing sugar
1 x 60 g egg

TOPPING
250 g Cadbury Dark Cooking chocolate, melted
60 g unsalted butter, melted
40 g copha, melted
250 g Pascal's marshmallows, cut into small pieces
75 g macadamia nuts
50 g whole glacé cherries

1 Preheat the oven to 180ºC (350ºF).
2 **TO MAKE BASE.** Rub the butter lightly through the sifted flour, cocoa and icing sugar until mixture resembles fresh breadcrumbs.
3 Add the egg and mix to a dough. Press dough into a 28 x 18 x 2 cm baking pan lined with baking paper. Bake for 10 minutes.
4 **TO MAKE TOPPING.** Mix the melted chocolate, butter and copha, then pour over the chopped marshmallows, macadamias and cherries.
5 Work quickly to combine all the ingredients together and then pour onto the cooled base.
6 Spread evenly, then allow to set in the refrigerator before cutting with a hot knife. Portions can then be stored in the refrigerator.

MAKES 16 PORTIONS

Rocky Road Slice

CHOCOLATE CREAM PUFFS

1 cup (250 ml) water

90 g unsalted butter

¾ cup (100 g) plain flour, sifted

1½ tablespoons (15 g) Cadbury Bournville Cocoa, sifted

4 to 5 x 60 g eggs

icing sugar or Cadbury Bournville Cocoa for dusting

1 quantity Creamy Chocolate Mousse

1 Preheat the oven to 200°C (400°F).

2 Place the water and butter in a saucepan and bring slowly to the boil. While the mixture is boiling, stir in the flour and cocoa. Continue stirring vigorously as the mixture cooks and until it leaves the sides of the pan and forms a solid ball (approximately 2 minutes).

3 Beat in four eggs one at a time until the mixture becomes smooth and shiny. Remove from heat. (If the mixture requires, add the last egg.) Stop beating. The mixture is ready when a knife run through it leaves a trail.

4 Place large tablespoons of the batter onto a lightly greased tray and bake in the oven for 35 to 40 minutes. To prevent steam from escaping, do not open the oven door for the first 15 minutes.

5 When baked, pierce a small hole in the base of each puff to allow internal steam to escape. Allow puffs to cool. Scoop out any uncooked mixture.

6 When cold cut in half and fill with Creamy Chocolate Mousse.

7 Dust the top with icing sugar or cocoa or a mixture of both.

MAKES 12

CHOCOLATE SUGAR DELIGHTS

180 g unsalted butter, softened

1 cup (180 g) brown sugar

3 tablespoons golden syrup

1 x 60 g egg

2 cups (250 g) plain flour

2 teaspoons baking powder

2 tablespoons Cadbury Bournville Cocoa

2 teaspoons cinnamon

raw sugar granules for rolling biscuits

1 Cream the butter, sugar and golden syrup together until light and fluffy. Add the egg and combine thoroughly.

2 Sift all the dry ingredients together and

add to the creamed butter mixture in two batches. Mix well. Cover the mixture and refrigerate for 45 minutes.

3 Preheat oven to 180°C (350°F).

4 Take walnut-sized portions of the mixture and roll into balls. Roll half of each ball in the raw sugar granules and place onto a tray lined with baking paper. Keep biscuits apart as they will spread considerably.

5 Bake for 10 to 12 minutes. Remove from the oven and allow to cool slightly on the tray before removing to a cooling wire.

MAKES 24 (APPROXIMATELY)

❖ CREAMY CHOCOLATE MOUSSE

120 g cream cheese

⅔ cup (150 g) caster sugar

2 x 60 g egg yolks

2½ cups (600 ml) thickened cream

125 g Cadbury Dark Cooking Chocolate, melted

125 g Cadbury Milk Cooking Chocolate, melted

1 Beat cream cheese, sugar and egg yolks until smooth.

2 Whip cream until stiff and return to refrigerator.

3 Quickly stir melted chocolates into cream cheese mixture and fold through whipped cream by hand.

4 Fill cream puffs.

Chocolate Cream Puffs

*Carefully remove pips
from fresh orange
segments before using in a
recipe, or for decorating or
filling.*

CHOC-ORANGE TORTLETS

*Choc-orange tortlets have
a moist texture when finished.*

3 whole oranges

6 x 60 g eggs, separated

1⅓ cups (300 g) caster sugar

300 g ground almonds

**4½ tablespoons Cadbury Bournville Cocoa,
sifted**

1 teaspoon baking powder

segments of 3 fresh oranges

50 g Unichoc White Buttons, melted

1 Preheat the oven to 180°C (350°F).

2 Grease and lightly flour two 5 cm muffin
or patty pans.

3 Place the whole oranges into a saucepan,
cover with hot water and slowly bring to the
boil. Boil for 1 hour. Keep topping up with
more water and do not allow them to boil
dry. After boiling, drain and purée the
oranges in a blender until they are a smooth
pulp.

4 Whisk the egg yolks and half the sugar
until thick and frothy.

5 Whisk the egg whites in a separate
mixing bowl until stiff and frothy and very
white. While continuing to whisk, slowly
add the remaining half of the caster sugar
until the sugar has dissolved.

6 Add the ground almonds, sifted cocoa
and baking powder to the egg whites and
fold through lightly.

7 Fold the egg yolk mixture into the
puréed oranges, then fold the egg white
mixture into the orange mixture a spoonful
at a time.

8 Three-quarter fill each of the muffin
moulds with the mixture and bake for
30 minutes or until each springs back to a
light touch.

9 Allow to cool in the patty pans for
10 minutes before removing carefully from
moulds and cooling on a cooling wire. When
cold, cut each of the cakes in half and fill
with fresh orange segments. Drizzle white
chocolate over the top of each cake and place
halves together immediately.

MAKES 24

ROCK CAKES

Rock cakes can be frozen.

150 g unsalted butter

¾ cup (180 g) caster sugar

½ cup (60 g) Cadbury Bournville Cocoa, sifted

1 x 60 g egg

3½ cups (450 g) plain flour

2 tablespoons baking powder

1¼ cups (50 g) shredded coconut

1 cup (250 ml) milk

100 g Cadbury Chocolate Dots

icing sugar for dusting

1 Preheat the oven to 200°C (400°F).

2 Line a baking tray with baking paper.

3 Cream the butter, sugar and sifted cocoa
together until light and fluffy. Add the egg
and continue mixing until combined.

4 Sift the flour and baking powder and add
to the coconut. Add half of the dry
ingredients to the butter mixture and stir
together with half of the milk, until
combined. Add the final half of both the
milk and the dry ingredients, as well as the
chocolate dots.

5 Place tablespoonfuls of mixture onto the
baking tray, leaving room between each for
spreading. Bake for 15 to 20 minutes or
until firm to touch.

6 Allow to cool on the tray before dusting
with icing sugar.

MAKES 40

CHOC-SPUDS

3 x 60 g eggs, separated
⅓ cup (90 g) caster sugar
¾ cup (90 g) plain flour, sifted
1 teaspoon cinnamon
1 tablespoon Cadbury Bournville Cocoa
2 cups (390 g) apricot jam
400 g marzipan
120 g slivered almonds
Cadbury Bournville Cocoa for dusting

1 Preheat the oven to 180°C (350°F).

2 Whisk the egg yolks and half of the sugar until light and fluffy.

3 Place the egg whites into another mixing bowl and whisk until white and frothy and stiff peaks have formed. Begin adding the other half of the sugar slowly and continue whisking until it is all dissolved.

4 Add the sifted flour, cinnamon and cocoa and half the egg white mixture to the egg yolk mix and fold through thoroughly. Add the other half of the egg whites carefully.

5 Using a piping bag fitted with a plain nozzle with a 1 cm opening, carefully pipe ovals approximately 5 cm in length x 3 cm in width onto a tray lined with baking paper. Bake for 20 minutes and then allow to cool on the tray.

6 Sandwich two of the cakes together with a little apricot jam and then coat the outsides with a little more jam.

7 Using small pieces at a time, roll out the marzipan thinly on a lightly cornfloured bench top. If it seems too hard to roll, work in the hands for a few minutes. Cut large enough circles from the thin marzipan to completely encase each of the jammed cakes. Wrap around tightly and pinch off the excess marzipan underneath.

8 Press several slivered almonds in the sides of each potato for eyes and then dust each with cocoa and serve.

MAKES 14

AFGHANS

200 g unsalted butter, softened
¾ cup (120 g) brown sugar, firmly packed
1 tablespoon clear honey
1 x 60 g egg
2¼ cups (270 g) plain flour
3 tablespoons Cadbury Bournville Cocoa
2 teaspoons baking powder
⅔ cup (60 g) desiccated coconut
1 teaspoon vanilla essence
2 ½ cups (75 g) cornflakes

ICING
¾ cup (120 g) icing sugar
2 tablespoons Cadbury Drinking Chocolate
3 to 4 teaspoons hot water
Cadbury Chocolate Dots

1 Preheat the oven to 180°C (350°F).

2 Cream the butter and sugar until light and fluffy. Add the honey and the egg and combine well.

3 Sift the flour, cocoa powder and baking powder and add to the mixture, then add the coconut and vanilla essence. Lastly add the cornflakes and mix lightly, taking care not to break them up.

4 Place heaped tablespoons of the mixture onto baking trays lined with baking paper, leaving room between each for spreading. Bake for 8 to 10 minutes.

5 When baked, remove biscuits to a wire cooling rack and drizzle 1 teaspoon of the chocolate icing over the top of each. Before this sets, sprinkle liberally with Chocolate Dots.

6 TO MAKE ICING. Sift together the icing sugar and the drinking chocolate and slowly add the water until a thick icing paste has formed. Use immediately.

MAKES 24 TO 30

Triple Chocolate Muffins and Chocolate Coconut Muffins

COCOA DIAMONDS

1½ cups (180 g) plain flour

1 teaspoon baking powder

3 tablespoons Cadbury Bournville Cocoa

⅔ cup (60 g) desiccated coconut

½ cup (120 g) caster sugar

125 g unsalted butter, melted

1 x 60 g egg, beaten

50 g whole blanched almonds

Cadbury Drinking Chocolate, for dusting

1 Preheat the oven to 180°C (350°F).

2 Lightly grease a 18 x 28 x 2 cm baking pan.

3 Sift together the flour, baking powder and cocoa. Add the coconut and sugar and mix together.

4 Add melted butter and the egg to the dry ingredients. Mix well.

5 Press the mixture into the prepared pan. Press in the whole almonds at regular intervals over the surface of the mixture.

6 Bake for 15 minutes. Allow to cool for 15 to 20 minutes in the pan before dusting with the drinking chocolate and cutting into diamond shapes.

MAKES 40 (APPROXIMATELY)

CHOCOLATE CHIP AND COCONUT MUFFINS

3¼ cups (390 g) plain flour
1 tablespoon baking powder
¾ cup (120 g) brown sugar
½ cup (120 g) caster sugar
100 g Cadbury Chocolate Dots
2½ cups (120 g) shredded coconut
1 ¼ cups (300 ml) milk
100 g butter, melted
2 x 60 g eggs, lightly beaten

1 Preheat the oven to 180°C (350°F).
2 Lightly grease a 5 cm muffin or patty pan.
3 Sift the flour and baking powder. Add the brown sugar, caster sugar, chocolate dots and coconut and stir lightly to combine all ingredients.
4 Add the milk, melted butter and eggs and mix through the dry ingredients until all are combined.
5 Three-quarter fill each of the muffin moulds with the mixture and bake for 20 minutes. When baked, cool muffins for 5 minutes, then remove each muffin carefully from the pan and cool on a cooling wire.

MAKES 15

CHOCOLATE SLICE

100 g unsalted butter, melted
1 ¼ cups (240 g) caster sugar
¾ cup (100 g) plain flour, sifted
60 g finely chopped pecan nuts
2 x 60 g eggs
3 tablespoons Cadbury Bournville Cocoa
icing sugar for dusting

1 Preheat the oven to 160°C (325°F).
2 Grease an 18 x 28 x 2 cm baking pan and line with baking paper.

3 Whisk all ingredients until well combined. Continue mixing for a further 5 minutes. Allow mix to rest slightly before pouring into prepared pan.
4 Bake for 20 to 25 minutes or until firm. Dust slice with icing sugar while still hot.
5 Allow to cool for 2 hours before cutting into portions.

MAKES 24 PORTIONS

TRIPLE CHOCOLATE MUFFINS

3 cups (360 g) plain flour
3 tablespoons Cadbury Bournville Cocoa
1 tablespoon baking powder
1½ cups (240 g) brown sugar
100 g Cadbury Chocolate Dots
100 g Cadbury White Cooking Chocolate, chopped
1 ¼ cups (300 ml) milk
120 g butter, melted
2 x 60 g eggs, lightly beaten

1 Preheat the oven to 160°C (325°F).
2 Grease a 5 cm muffin or patty pan.
3 Sift the flour, cocoa and baking powder. Add the brown sugar, chocolate dots and chopped white chocolate. Then add the milk, melted butter and eggs and mix through the dry ingredients until all are combined.
4 Three-quarter fill each of the muffin moulds and bake for 20 to 25 minutes. When baked, allow the muffins to cool in the pan for 10 minutes before carefully removing each muffin from the pan and cooling on a cake wire.

MAKES 15

✥ **MUFFIN PANS**
Muffin pans are available in 6, 12 and 18 hole pans and can be bought according to the size of the muffin required. These can be 4 to 5 cm or 9 to 10 cm.

SWEET AND SAUCY

What good would a dessert, ice cream or slice of cake be if it was served without a rich, seductive and alluring coating of chocolate sauce. Try them all and choose your favourite.

The Step-by-Step Technique in this chapter shows the making of *The Ultimate Chocolate Sauce.*

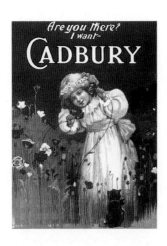

The Ultimate Chocolate Sauce

WHITE CHOCOLATE SAUCE

60 g unsalted butter

½ cup (125 ml) thickened cream

½ cup (120 g) caster sugar

250 g Cadbury White Cooking Chocolate, chopped

1 Gently heat butter and cream until butter has melted.

2 Add the sugar and slowly bring the mixture to the boil. Then add the chopped chocolate and remove the saucepan from the heat. Stir until the chocolate has melted.

3 Serve immediately.

MAKES 2 CUPS (APPROXIMATELY)

HOT CHOCOLATE FUDGE

60 g unsalted butter

120 g Cadbury Milk Cooking Chocolate, chopped

¼ cup (60 g) caster sugar

½ cup (125 ml) thickened cream

1 Place butter and chopped chocolate into the top of a double boiler and stir until completely melted.

2 Add the sugar to the melted mixture and stir until dissolved, then add the cream and stir again until well combined.

3 The hot chocolate fudge should be served warm.

MAKES 1 ½ CUPS (APPROXIMATELY)

From top: White Chocolate Sauce,
Hot Chocolate Fudge, Chocolate Custard

CHOCOLATE CUSTARD

⅔ cup (150 g) caster sugar

6 tablespoons Cadbury Bournville Cocoa, sifted

3 tablespoons cornflour, sifted

2 cups (500 ml) milk

1 ¼ cups (300 ml) thickened cream

1 teaspoon vanilla essence

2 x 60 g eggs

1 Place all ingredients into a saucepan and whisk together to remove any lumps.
2 Gently heat for approximately 5 minutes or until the mixture begins to thicken. Continue to stir and increase the heat to allow the mixture to come to the boil.
3 Remove from heat and strain into a serving bowl or into individual bowls.

MAKES 4 CUPS (APPROXIMATELY)

LIQUEUR SENSATION

1 ¼ cups (300 ml) water

½ cup (120 g) caster sugar

100 g Cadbury Dark Cooking Chocolate, chopped

165 g Cadbury Milk Cooking Chocolate, chopped

⅓ cup Amaretto liqueur

1 ½ tablespoons cognac

1 Bring the water and sugar to the boil in a saucepan.
2 Add the boiled liquid to the chopped chocolate and stir until melted and the mixture is smooth.
3 Add the Amaretto and cognac to the cooling sauce and serve immediately for the best taste.

MAKES 4 CUPS (APPROXIMATELY)

From top: Liqueur Sensation,
Chocolate Crème Anglaise, Sweet Seduction

CHOCOLATE CRÉME ANGLAISE

1 cup (250 ml) milk

1 cup (250 ml) thickened cream

6 x 60 g egg yolks

⅓ cup (90 g) caster sugar

120 g Cadbury Milk Cooking Chocolate

1 Bring the milk and cream slowly to the boil in a saucepan.

2 Mix together the egg yolks and the sugar in a large bowl.

3 Melt the chocolate over a double boiler.

4 When the milk and cream have boiled, slowly pour over the egg yolk mixture while whisking quickly. When all the boiled liquid has been blended, pour the liquid back into the saucepan. Stir the liquid slowly with a wooden spoon over a low heat until the liquid begins to thicken and coat the back of the wooden spoon. Do not allow to boil or a curdle will result. Remove from heat.

5 Slowly pour in the melted chocolate, whisking until it is completely blended.

MAKES 3 CUPS (APPROXIMATELY)

QUICK CHOCOLATE SAUCE

2½ cups (600 ml) thickened cream

250 g Cadbury Dark Cooking Chocolate, chopped

1½ tablespoons rum (optional)

1 Place all ingredients into a saucepan and stir over a low heat. Heat until chocolate is melted and all ingredients are combined into a smooth sauce.

2 Serve immediately.

MAKES 3 CUPS (APPROXIMATELY)

SWEET SEDUCTION

1 cup (250 ml) water

⅔ cup (150 g) caster sugar

250 g Cadbury Milk Cooking Chocolate, chopped

30 g unsalted butter

1 Bring the water and sugar to the boil in a saucepan.

2 Add the chopped chocolate and butter to the boiling water and stir until all ingredients are melted and well combined.

MAKES 2½ CUPS (APPROXIMATELY)

FONDUE

½ cup (150 g) glucose syrup

⅔ cup (150 ml) thickened cream

250 g Cadbury Dark Cooking Chocolate, chopped

selection of fresh fruits

1 Gently heat the glucose and the cream in a saucepan and stir until boiled.

2 Remove from the heat and add the chopped chocolate and stir until all ingredients are combined.

3 Serve immediately with a selection of fresh fruits, each marinated in your favourite liqueur.

MAKES 2 CUPS (APPROXIMATELY)

✤ **MOCHA FONDUE**
For a fondue with a kick, add 2 to 3 tablespoons of Tia Maria (coffee liqueur) and serve with Savoiardi Sponge Biscuits, and some good, strong Italian coffee.

Icecream with Quick Chocolate Sauce

CREATIVE CONFECTIONERY

If your chocolate cravings are of the twenty four-hour variety, then keep a jar of each of these sweet treats on hand so you can nibble at will.

The Step-by-Step Technique in this chapter shows chocolate being used as a binding medium in the *Dark Chocolate Fudge*.

Dark Chocolate Fudge and White Chocolate Fudge

STEP-BY-STEP TECHNIQUES

Combine all ingredients in a saucepan and slowly bring to boil, stirring continuously.

Remove from heat and continue stirring.

DARK CHOCOLATE FUDGE

2¼ cups (480 g) caster sugar

1¼ cups (300 ml) thickened cream

120 g Unichoc Dark Buttons

1 tablespoon liquid glucose

15 g butter

1 Combine all ingredients in a large saucepan and allow mixture to dissolve over a gentle heat. Bring mixture slowly to boil, stirring continuously and allow to boil for 6 minutes.

2 Remove saucepan from the heat and continue stirring until bubbles subside. Allow mixture to cool. When cool, beat vigorously until mixture loses shine.

3 Spread into a foil-lined tray and refrigerate until set.

MAKES 30 SQUARES

Dark Chocolate Fudge and White Chocolate Fudge

CHRISTMAS LOGS

⅓ cup (85 ml) thickened cream

250 g Cadbury Milk Cooking Chocolate, melted

300 g green coloured marzipan or almond paste

100 g Unichoc Dark Buttons, melted

icing sugar for dusting

1 Make a ganache by bringing the cream to the boil in a saucepan, then remove from the heat and immediately add the milk chocolate and stir until smooth.

2 Place in the fridge and stir until the paste becomes firm enough to pipe.

3 Roll out the marzipan in a square shape to ½ cm in thickness on a lightly floured bench.

4 Place the ganache into a piping bag fitted with a 1 cm plain nozzle and pipe lines of the chocolate mixture onto the marzipan. For the first line leave 2 cm from the top edge of the marzipan and when piped leave 2 cm gap before the next line of chocolate mixture. When finished piping, cut the marzipan down the centre between each piped line.

5 Place in the refrigerator to harden for 5 to 10 minutes.

6 Roll the marzipan around the chocolate mixture and roll on the bench to force the join to close up. Cut off any excess marzipan to use as another log.

7 Brush the melted dark chocolate over the outsides of the marzipan to give each roll a good coating. Allow this to set on foil before cutting 2 to 3 cm lengths from the log.

8 Dust lightly with icing sugar before serving.

MAKES 35 TO 40

WHITE CHOCOLATE FUDGE

2½ cups (500 g) caster sugar

1¼ cups (300 ml) thickened cream

15 g unsalted butter

120 g Unichoc White Buttons

1 tablespoon liquid glucose syrup

100 g Unichoc White Buttons, extra, melted

1 Combine the sugar, cream, butter and chocolate in a large saucepan with the glucose and allow the mix to dissolve over a gentle heat.

2 Bring the mixture slowly to the boil, stirring continuously and boil for 7 minutes or until golden brown in colour.

3 Remove the saucepan from the heat and continue stirring until the bubbles subside. Allow the mixture to cool.

4 When cooled to lukewarm, beat vigorously until the mixture loses its shine, spread into a foil-lined tray and refrigerate until set.

5 Cut into small squares and drizzle with melted white chocolate.

MAKES 24 SQUARES

✥ **TINTING MARZIPAN**

Flatten the piece of marzipan to be coloured and add a drop of food colouring to the centre. Fold the marzipan to enclose the colouring. Lightly knead the marzipan until the colouring is completely absorbed. Continue to add food colouring drop by drop until the required colour is achieved.

ALMOND SWIRLS

2½ cups (300 g) plain flour, sifted

1 cup (150 g) icing sugar, sifted

1 teaspoon cinnamon

150 g unsalted butter

1 x 60 g egg yolk

1 tablespoon water

GANACHE

½ cup (125 ml) thickened cream

2½ tablespoons Grand Marnier liqueur or orange juice

500 g Cadbury Dark Cooking Chocolate, chopped

100 g roasted whole blanched almonds

1 Lightly rub the flour, icing sugar, cinnamon and butter together until the mixture resembles coarse breadcrumbs. Add the egg and the water and work the mixture to a dough. Wrap in cling film and refrigerate for 1 hour.

2 Preheat the oven to 180°C (350°F).

3 When chilled, remove and knead lightly until dough is soft enough to roll. Roll the dough to 2 to 3 mm in thickness on a lightly floured bench. Cut small circles from the rolled paste (2 to 3 cm in diameter) using a fluted round cutter.

4 Place the biscuits directly onto lightly greased baking trays and bake 8 to 12 minutes or until light golden brown.

5 **TO MAKE GANACHE.** Place the cream and Grand Marnier in a saucepan and bring to the boil. When boiling, immediately add the chopped chocolate, then remove pan from the heat and stir until well combined.

6 Allow the chocolate mixture to cool slightly and then place it in the refrigerator, stirring every few minutes until the mix is thick enough to pipe.

7 Take each biscuit one at a time and pipe a neat rosette of the chocolate ganache onto the smooth (bottom) side. Place a roasted whole almond on top of each rosette, in the centre.

MAKES 40 TO 50

MARZIPAN CHOCOLATE

½ cup (120 g) caster sugar

¾ cup (120 g) icing sugar, sifted

1½ tablespoons cornflour

3 tablespoons Cadbury Bournville Cocoa

240 g ground almonds

1 x 60 g egg, lightly beaten

375 g Unichoc Dark Buttons, melted

200 g roasted flaked almonds

1 Mix together the caster sugar, icing sugar, cornflour, cocoa and the ground almonds.

2 Slowly add the lightly beaten egg and mix until the mixture forms a pliable dough. If the mix seems a little dry add some more egg; if it feels a little moist add more icing sugar to stiffen the dough.

3 Cut the dough into four pieces and roll each piece into a sausage shape of 1 cm in diameter and cut into 3 cm lengths.

4 Dip each of these into the melted chocolate and then immediately roll in roasted flaked almonds. Place dipped and rolled pieces onto a paper-lined tray and place into refrigerator until chocolate has hardened.

MAKES 48

❖ **ROASTING ALMONDS**

Preheat oven to 180°C (350°F). Spread almonds thinly on a baking tray. Bake for 4 minutes, then turn with a fork. Bake another 4 minutes, then turn again. Continue this process until almonds are golden brown. Cool on tray. Roasted almonds can be stored in an airtight container for up to 2 weeks.

Almond Swirls

STEP-BY-STEP TECHNIQUES

CHOCOLATE PRETZELS

3 tablespoons Cadbury Bournville Cocoa

2½ tablespoons boiling water

125 g unsalted butter

¼ cup (60 g) caster sugar

1 x 60 g egg

2 cups (250 g) plain flour, sifted

375 g Unichoc Dark Buttons, melted

1 Line a flat baking sheet with baking paper.

2 Stir the cocoa powder into boiling water until a paste is formed and no lumps remain.

3 Cream the butter and the sugar together until light and fluffy. Add the egg and beat in well. Then add the cocoa paste and flour and work the mixture to a soft dough. Wrap in cling film and chill for 1 hour.

4 Preheat the oven to 180°C (350°F).

5 Lightly knead the chilled dough until soft enough to roll by hand. Take small amounts at a time and roll them into sausage shapes ½ cm in thickness and 15 cm in length. Place shapes onto the lined tray.

6 Take both ends of the sausage and draw them up towards you so that they meet in the middle. Cross the two ends over and then draw them back into the base of the shape to form a pretzel. Continue shaping the dough in this way.

7 Bake the finished biscuits for 8 to 10 minutes. Allow the pretzels to cool on the baking tray before dipping them in the melted chocolate. Drain them slightly, return them to the lined tray and place in the refrigerator to set.

MAKES 12 TO 18

Roll dough into sausage shapes 5 cm thick and 15 cm long.

Take both ends of sausage and draw them up to the middle then cross ends over to form a pretzel.

Chocolate Pretzels

CHOCOLATE PÂTÉ

120 g shortbread biscuits

180 g Cadbury Dark Cooking Chocolate

⅓ cup (100 ml) water

¾ cup (180 g) caster sugar

1 tablespoon Cadbury Bournville Cocoa

180 g unsalted butter

60 g brazil nuts, chopped

60 g pistachio nuts (approximately 110 g with shells), chopped

60 g glacé pineapple, chopped

60 g glacé apricots, chopped

2½ tablespoons Grand Marnier

zest of 1 orange

zest of 1 lemon

1 x 60 g egg

2 x egg yolks

1 Crush the biscuits finely and melt the chocolate.

2 Bring the water and sugar in a saucepan slowly to the boil and boil for 5 minutes. Allow to cool slightly.

3 Cream the cocoa and butter together until light and fluffy. Mix the chopped nuts, fruits and crushed biscuits.

4 Add the chocolate to the boiled sugar syrup and stir till smooth, then add the Grand Marnier, lemon and orange zests and finally the egg and egg yolks.

5 Fold in the butter/cocoa mix, fruit, nuts and biscuit mixture and stir until well combined.

6 Line a 23 cm springform cake tin with cling film and pour in the mixture. Press firmly into the tin and smooth the top.

7 Refrigerate for 24 hours before unmoulding and serving in very fine slices with coffee.

SERVES 20

CHOCOLATE TRUFFLES

⅓ cup (90 ml) thickened cream

50 g unsalted butter

250 g Cadbury Dark Cooking Chocolate, chopped

1½ tablespoons Grand Marnier liqueur, or zest of 1 orange

Cadbury Drinking Chocolate for dusting

1 Bring the cream and butter in a saucepan slowly to the boil. Add the chocolate and mix to a smooth liquid, then add the Grand Marnier and stir in well.

2 Pour the mixture into a stainless steel bowl and place in the refrigerator. Stir every few minutes until the mixture becomes smooth and thick enough to pipe.

3 Fill a piping bag (with a 1½ cm star piping nozzle) with the truffle mixture. Pipe star or rosette shapes onto a tray lined with baking paper. When the tray is full, place into the refrigerator and allow truffles to set hard.

4 Remove and dust each with the drinking chocolate. Place onto a serving dish and serve immediately. If not for immediate use, then place coated truffles in an airtight container and store in the refrigerator until required.

MAKES 35 (APPROXIMATELY)

✤ LEMON AND ORANGE ZEST

A lemon zester is a useful and impressive piece of equipment. It is designed to extract the outer zest from the lemon or orange, leaving the white pith behind.

The smallest grate-size of a grater is a substitute but be careful not to grate any pith into the zest.

✜ CREATIVE PACKAGING

You can package your creations in many different ways. Put pieces of Dark Chocolate Fudge and White Chocolate Fudge in a little cellophane bag and tie with coloured ribbons. Buy colourful boxes in interesting shapes from a gift shop or department store and put Whisky Wonder Balls or Chocolate Pretzels inside. Or make your own: make boxes from cardboard and cover with gift wrap, fabric, or paper which you have decorated yourself. Filled with irresistible chocolate treats, these make wonderful gifts for all occasions.

WICKED AND WITTY

Chocolate should always be taken seriously. However, the way it is served to you should not.

The Step-by-Step Technique in this chapter shows the making of a *Jack O'Lantern* using chocolate for rich flavour.

Halloween Cake with Jack o' Lanterns

STEP-BY-STEP TECHNIQUES

Cut circles in the rolled out marzipan.

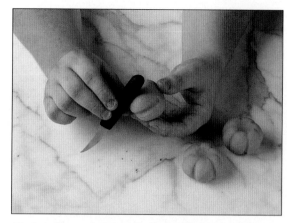

Mark six lines around the sides of each ball, from top to bottom using a knife handle or the side of a pen.

Quickly place a ball on each disk of marzipan and wrap tightly, pinching off any excess marzipan.

Press down on the top of each ball to indent slightly, then cut out eyes, nose and mouth.

JACK O'LANTERNS

210 g sponge crumbs

2 tablespoons Cadbury Drinking Chocolate

2 tablespoons Cadbury Bournville Cocoa

½ cup (45 g) desiccated coconut

45 g ground almonds

100 g chopped walnuts

2 tablespoons Grand Marnier

2 tablespoons butter, melted

2 tablespoons (60 g) apricot jam

420 g orange coloured marzipan/almond paste/plastic icing

60 g green coloured marzipan

1 Place all the ingredients except the marzipans into a bowl and crumble together until the mixture forms a soft dough or paste. Divide the mixture into twelve portions and roll each into a ball and refrigerate for 30 minutes.

2 Roll the orange marzipan to a thickness of 2 mm and using a cutter which is approximately double the size in diameter as the balls cut out twelve circles. Quickly place one ball onto each disc of marzipan and wrap each ball tightly, pinching off any excess marzipan from the base.

3 Hold each ball and mark 6 lines around the sides of the ball, using the handle of a knife or the side of a pen.

4 Place the balls onto a flat surface and using the thumb press down slightly on the top of each ball to give a slight indent where all the lines have met.

5 Cut out two triangles for eyes from one side of the ball and a triangular nose below that, and then mark in a jagged mouth with a sharp knife or a small triangular marzipan modelling tool. Into the top of the indentation press a little piece of green marzipan which has been rolled into a small sausage shape.

6 Refrigerate well before serving.

MAKES 12

Jack O' Lantern

HALLOWEEN CAKE

150 g unsalted butter

1 cup (150 g) brown sugar

2 x 60 g eggs

1¾ cups (210 g) plain flour

4½ tablespoons Cadbury Bournville Cocoa

2 teaspoons baking powder

¾ cup (185 ml) milk

45 g ground almonds

½ cup (45 g) desiccated coconut

300 g carton sour cream

TOPPING

½ cup (125 ml) thickened cream

250 g Cadbury Dark Cooking Chocolate, chocolate

12 x Jack O'Lanterns

1 Lightly grease a 22 cm round springform cake pan.

2 Preheat the oven to 180°C (350°F).

3 Cream the butter and sugar until light and fluffy. Add the eggs one at a time and mix well between additions. Then add the sifted flour, cocoa and baking powder along with the milk, ground almonds, coconut and sour cream and mix until the batter is smooth.

4 Spread the mixture evenly into the prepared pan and bake for 50 to 60 minutes in the preheated oven or until cooked.

5 Allow the cake to cool in the pan for 10 minutes before removing carefully to a cooling wire.

6 TO MAKE TOPPING. Bring the cream to the boil and add the chocolate, stir till smooth and then allow to cool slightly.

7 When the cake is cool, pour the chocolate coating over the top of the cake and spread to cover the top and sides of the cake. Allow the cake to sit for several minutes to allow excess coating to drip off, then refrigerate it for 20 minutes.

8 Prepare the Jack O'Lanterns either while the cake cooks or cools, then place them around the sides of the cake, serving 1 per portion for a truly devilish dessert.

SERVES 12

Christmas Puddings

CHRISTMAS PUDDINGS

⊹ MARZIPAN ALTERNATIVE

In any recipe where marzipan is required, it can be replaced by ready-roll fondant or self-roll icing, available at supermarkets.

PUDDING

½ cup (125 ml) thickened cream

360 g Cadbury Dark Cooking Chocolate, chopped

2 ½ tablespoons Grand Marnier liqueur or orange juice

BASE

60 g unsalted butter

¾ cup (100 g) plain flour, sifted

1 ½ tablespoons Cadbury Bournville Cocoa

¼ cup (45 g) icing sugar

2 egg yolks

240 g Unichoc White Buttons, melted

90 g marzipan coloured with green food colouring

30 g marzipan coloured with red food colouring

1 TO MAKE PUDDING. Place the cream into a saucepan and bring slowly to the boil. Add the chopped chocolate and Grand Marnier and stir until the mixture becomes thick and smooth. Pour into a baking tray and refrigerate the mixture until it becomes very hard.

2 TO MAKE BASE. Rub butter into the flour, cocoa and icing sugar until mixture resembles fine breadcrumbs. Add egg yolk and mix thoroughly. Cover and allow the dough to rest for 5 minutes.

3 Roll the dough thinly on a lightly floured bench surface and using a 3 cm round fluted cutter cut out approximately 14 circles.

4 Remove the chilled and solid chocolate mixture and cut it into strips. Cut the strips into 2 cm lengths and roll each into a ball. Place each ball onto a base circle. (If the chocolate mixture becomes a little soft to roll, place into the freezer section for several minutes.)

5 Pipe a little melted white chocolate onto the top of each pudding and allow it to run slightly down the sides of the puddings.

6 Make little leaves or holly leaves by pinching little pieces of the green marzipan. Place two leaves onto the white chocolate. Roll very tiny little balls for the holly berries with the red marzipan and place three little balls per pudding on top beside the leaves.

7 Chill for 20 minutes before serving.

MAKES 14

CHOCOLATE MOUSSE MICE

FILLING

1¼ cups (300 ml) thickened cream

120 g Cadbury White Cooking Chocolate, chopped

250 g Cadbury Dark Cooking Chocolate, chopped

BASE

150 g unsalted butter

1½ cups (180 g) plain flour

½ cup (75 g) sifted icing sugar

3 tablespoons Cadbury Bournville Cocoa, sifted

1 x 60 g egg yolk

375 g Unichoc Dark Buttons, melted

90 g Unichoc White Buttons, melted

flaked almonds for ears

1 TO MAKE FILLING. Make the filling the night before so that it can set firm. Place the cream into a saucepan and bring to the boil. Add the chopped chocolates and stir until the mixture is smooth. Refrigerate the chocolate mixture overnight.

2 Preheat the oven to 180°C (350°F).

3 TO MAKE BASE BISCUITS. Rub the butter lightly through the sifted flour, icing sugar and cocoa until the mixture resembles coarse breadcrumbs. Add the egg yolk and work the mixture to a dough. Wrap and refrigerate the dough for 30 minutes.

4 Roll out the chilled dough on a lightly floured bench surface to approximately 2 mm in thickness and using a tear drop cutter (5 or 6 cm in length) or template or freehand cut out teardrop shaped biscuits.

5 Bake biscuits for 10 to 12 minutes then allow to cool on the tray.

6 Remove the chilled chocolate mixture from the refrigerator and using a wooden spoon stir the mix quickly until it stiffens into a pipeable mixture. Place the chocolate mix into a pastry bag fitted with a 1 cm plain nozzle.

7 Take one of the cooled biscuits and starting at the round end pipe a bulb of chocolate mixture to cover the biscuit, then pull the piping bag away slowly down towards the pointed end.

8 When all biscuits and chocolate mixture have been used, place the mousse-covered biscuits in the refrigerator for 30 minutes.

9 About 2 to 3 cm back from the pointiest end of the mousse-covered biscuits press two pieces of flaked almonds for ears and then quickly dip each mouse into the melted dark chocolate. Place back in the refrigerator to set firm.

10 When set, pipe the white chocolate on to each mouse to indicate eyes, nose and the tail.

MAKES 12 TO 18

✥ TEARDROP TEMPLATE

Use this teardrop template to shape the base biscuits for your chocolate mousse mice.

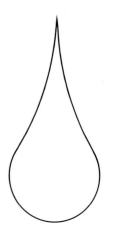

RUM BOYS

BASE

1½ cups (180 g) plain flour, sifted

½ cup (75 g) icing sugar, sifted

3 tablespoons Cadbury Bournville Cocoa, sifted

150 g unsalted butter

1 x 60 g egg yolk

RUM BALL TOPPING

210 g sponge crumbs

3 tablespoons Cadbury Bournville Cocoa

1 cup (90 g) desiccated coconut

90 g chopped unsalted peanuts

2 tablespoons brown rum

2 tablespoons unsalted butter

4 tablespoons apricot jam

TO DECORATE

375 g Unichoc Dark Buttons, melted

390 g almond paste or marzipan

1 Preheat oven to 180°C (350°F)

2 **TO MAKE BASE BISCUITS.** Lightly rub the sifted flour, icing sugar and cocoa with the butter until the mixture resembles coarse breadcrumbs.

3 Add the egg yolk and work the mixture to a dough. Wrap and refrigerate the dough for 30 minutes. Roll the chilled dough out on a lightly floured bench surface to approximately 2 to 3 mm in thickness and using a 4 cm round fluted cutter cut out biscuit bases.

4 Bake the biscuits for 12 minutes in preheated oven. Allow to cool.

5 **TO MAKE RUM BALL TOPPING.** Place all the ingredients for the rum ball mixture into a bowl and stir until the mixture comes together.

6 Press 90 g of the rum ball mixture onto each biscuit base and whilst pressing it firmly onto the base also shape it upwards to form a column 4 to 5 cm in height.

7 Place all topped biscuits into the refrigerator for 10 minutes.

8 **TO DECORATE.** Divide the marzipan into as many portions as there are biscuits. From each portion of marzipan, roll one large ball for a head, two small balls for ears, one ball for a nose and flatten a ball of coloured marzipan for a beret hat. Also make two balls (the size of a pea) per base and roll them into pear shapes for arms.

9 Remove the bases from the refrigerator and dip them one at a time into the melted chocolate. As soon as each one is covered with chocolate place one of the heads on top of the wet chocolate and press the two arms onto the sides of the body before the chocolate has set. Press two eyes and a mouth into the heads of the finished Rum Boys and if required pipe eyes into the sockets using a little white and dark chocolate.

MAKES 12 (APPROXIMATELY)

WHISKY WONDER BALLS

7 oz   210 g sponge crumbs

3 tablespoons Cadbury Drinking Chocolate

1 tablespoon Cadbury Bournville Cocoa

6 oz.   1 cup (90 g) desiccated coconut

4 oz   90 g roasted flaked almonds

3 tablespoons Scotch Whisky

1½ oz   30 g unsalted butter

2 tablespoons apricot jam

13 oz   375 g Unichoc Dark Buttons, melted

9 oz   250 g Cadbury Dark Cooking Chocolate, grated

1 Mix all the ingredients, except chocolates, by hand until they come together. (Depending on the moisture of the sponge, the mix may need more alcohol if it is too dry or more coconut if it is too wet).

2 Take heaped tablespoonfuls of the mixture and roll into balls, and place them onto a tray in the refrigerator for 5 minutes.

3 Melt the dark buttons, and grate the other chocolate putting it in a separate bowl ready to use.

4 Roll each of the balls by hand in the melted chocolate, drain, and then place directly into the grated chocolate and have a second person roll the balls to ensure an even covering.

5 Milk and white grated chocolate can be substituted for dark chocolate for rolling.

MAKES 24 (APPROXIMATELY)

Whisky Wonder Balls

OVER THE TOP

If you wouldn't go out for dinner undressed, then how can you possibly dream of serving up a chocolate creation uncovered. Each of these recipes has been chosen for its compatibility with just about every cake imaginable. Each recipe adds a little bit more to your creations.

The Step-by-Step Technique in this chapter shows chocolate used as a coating in making *White Butter Delight*.

From bottom, clockwise: Chocolate Ganache Glaze, Boiled Chocolate Glaze, Whipped Ganache, Chocolate Water Icing, White Butter Delight, Buttercream, Chocolate Frosting, Wicked Chocolate Cream

BUTTERCREAMS

In this section is a recipe for a simple chocolate buttercream. However, try the following recipes for something different. Simple or more complicated, light or rich, it is only by experimenting that you will discover which one you prefer.

STORAGE.

It is best to use buttercream as soon as it is made, when it is light, airy and fresh. If buttercream has to be stored it should be kept in an airtight container in the refrigerator. Remove from the refrigerator when required and stand at room temperature for one hour to soften. Beat in a mixing bowl until light and fluffy. Never make more buttercream than is required, to save time on the next cake. It is quicker to make it fresh than to reconstitute chilled buttercream. Never store buttercream for more than two weeks in the refrigerator.

CHOCOLATE GERMAN BUTTERCREAM

This is a light, sweet buttercream.

300 g unsalted butter
160 g (1 cup) icing sugar
¾ cup (200 ml) milk
¼ cup (50 g) caster sugar
¼ cup (60 ml) milk, extra
½ cup (50 g) custard powder
4 x 60 g eggs
120 g Cadbury Dark Cooking Chocolate, melted
1½ tablespoons (30 g) caster sugar, extra

1 Beat the butter and icing sugar until light, fluffy and pale yellow.
2 Place the milk and caster sugar in a saucepan and bring to the boil.
3 Blend the extra milk with the custard powder and eggs.
4 Pour the hot milk over the custard mixture, stirring all the time. Return to the saucepan and cook over a medium heat until thickened. Do not allow to boil. Remove from heat and stir in melted chocolate.
5 Pour into a shallow dish, sprinkle with the extra caster sugar to prevent a skin from forming and chill quickly.
6 When the custard is cool, beat into the creamed butter and icing sugar a spoonful at a time. Beat for 10 minutes.

MAKES ENOUGH TO COVER ONE 23 CM CAKE

CHOCOLATE FRENCH BUTTERCREAM

This is a heavy, rich buttercream, made with fondant which is available in ready-made tubs from supermarkets and delicatessens.

450 g unsalted butter
160 g fondant, softened
3 x 60 g eggs
100 g Cadbury Dark Cooking Chocolate, melted and cooled

1 Place butter and fondant into a mixing bowl and beat until white, fluffy and smooth.
2 Add the eggs one at a time and beat until thoroughly mixed.
3 Add the cooled, melted chocolate to the buttercream and beat until well mixed, but still fluffy.

MAKES ENOUGH TO COVER ONE 23 CM CAKE

STEP-BY-STEP TECHNIQUES

Add chocolate to the boiled milk and stir until melted. Add sugar and stir until dissolved.

Vary this icing by adding shredded orange and chocolate dots.

Stir chocolate mixture into the soft butter in 3 to 4 batches, stirring until the mixture is just combined each time.

Make a Mocha Butter Delight by adding coffee and Tia Maria to this icing.

WHITE BUTTER DELIGHT

½ cup (110 ml) milk

125 g Cadbury White Cooking Chocolate, chopped

¼ cup (60 g) caster sugar

1 x 60 g egg yolk

120 g butter, softened to room temperature

1 Place the milk in a saucepan and allow to come slowly to the boil.

2 Remove from the heat and immediately add the chocolate, stirring until melted, then add the sugar and continue stirring until it is dissolved. Add the egg yolk and stir well until combined. Allow mixture to cool to room temperature (almost cold).

3 Using a wooden spoon, stir the chocolate mixture into the soft butter in three to four amounts, stirring only until the mixture is just combined each time. When all of the chocolate mixture has been stirred through, allow the mixture to sit for 5 minutes before using for decorating.

**MAKES ENOUGH TO COVER
ONE 23 CM CAKE**

BROWNIES

250 g unsalted butter

180 g Cadbury Dark Cooking Chocolate

100 g Cadbury White Cooking Chocolate

1 cup (150 g) brown sugar

⅔ cup (150 g) caster sugar

1½ tablespoons golden syrup

1½ tablespoons honey

3 x 60 g eggs

1¼ cups (150 g) plain flour, sifted

300 g chopped macadamia nuts

1 cup (90 g) desiccated coconut

icing sugar for dusting

1 Preheat oven to 150°C (300°F).

2 Grease a 25 x 30 x 3 cm baking pan and line with baking paper.

3 Melt the butter and both the chocolates in a bowl over a saucepan of boiling water (double boiler). Remove from the heat and stir in the sugar, golden syrup and honey. Then stir in the eggs one at a time, followed by the flour, macadamia nuts and coconut.

4 Pour the mixture into the prepared pan and bake for 30 minutes or until firm to touch.

5 Cool in the pan and dust with icing sugar before cutting to serve.

MAKES 25 TO 30 PORTIONS

✥ **DELIGHTFUL BROWNIES**

For a treat that's hard to resist, make some delicious chocolate brownies, sandwich two together with White Butter Delight and spread it on top as well.

Chocolate Brownies with White Butter Delight

CHOCOLATE BUTTERCREAM

300 g unsalted butter, softened

¾ cup (135 g) icing sugar, sifted

2 x 60 g eggs

100 g Cadbury Dark Cooking Chocolate, melted

1 teaspoon vanilla essence

1 Cream the butter and sugar until light, fluffy and pale. Add the eggs one at a time and beat well after each addition.

2 Add the melted chocolate and stir in quickly before the chocolate sets or becomes hard.

3 Add the vanilla essence and continue beating for a further 10 minutes at medium speed until the mixture is light and creamy.

MAKES ENOUGH TO COVER ONE 23 CM CAKE

WICKED CHOCOLATE CREAM

¾ cup (200 ml) thickened cream

60 g unsalted butter

2 tablespoons sifted icing sugar

120 g Cadbury Milk Cooking Chocolate, chopped

1 Place the cream and butter into a saucepan and allow to slowly come to the boil. Remove saucepan from heat and add the remaining ingredients and stir until mixed.

2 Refrigerate the mixture until cold.

3 Whisk the cream until stiff and use immediately.

MAKES ENOUGH TO COVER ONE 23 CM CAKE

CHOCOLATE WATER ICING

1½ cups (240 g) icing sugar

3 tablespoons Cadbury Bournville Cocoa

2 to 3 tablespoons (50 ml) boiling water

1 Sift the icing sugar and cocoa into a bowl.

2 Add a little of the warm water at a time, firstly to make a stiff paste and then to thin it down to the required thickness.

3 Spread onto slices or cakes using a warm wet knife to give a smooth finish.

MAKES ENOUGH TO COVER ONE 23 CM CAKE

WHIPPED GANACHE

¾ cup (200 ml) thickened cream

60 g unsalted butter

500 g Cadbury Milk Cooking Chocolate, chopped

1 Place the cream and butter into a saucepan and slowly bring to the boil. Remove the boiling liquid from the heat and quickly stir through the chopped chocolate, stirring until the chocolate is melted and the mixture is thick and smooth.

2 Allow the mixture to cool to room temperature and then place into the refrigerator. Stir the mixture every 5 minutes until it becomes quite thick and hard to stir.

3 Beat the ganache with an electric mixer until it has increased in volume and has lightened in colour quite considerably. (If the mixture looks as if it may curdle at any stage, place the bowl into a pot of warm water and allow the mix to melt slightly. Then continue whipping with an electric mixer).

4 Spread immediately over any cakes or biscuits.

MAKES ENOUGH TO COVER ONE 23 CM CAKE

CHOCOLATE GANACHE GLAZE

⅔ cup (150 ml) thickened cream

30 g unsalted butter

500 g Cadbury Dark Cooking Chocolate, chopped

1 Place the cream and butter into a saucepan and slowly bring to the boil.

2 Add the chopped chocolate to the boiling liquid, remove from heat and stir until all the chocolate has melted and the mixture is thick and smooth.

3 Pour immediately over cakes or pastries which require coating.

MAKES ENOUGH TO COVER ONE 23 CM CAKE

BOILED CHOCOLATE GLAZE

1 cup (270 g) caster sugar

210 g Cadbury Dark Cooking Chocolate, chopped

⅔ cup (150 ml) water

1 Place all ingredients into a saucepan and slowly bring to the boil stirring continuously.

2 Boil for 6 minutes, making sure that the mixture does not catch on the bottom.

3 Allow to cool slightly before pouring over glazed or marzipan-covered cakes. Refrigerate until firm before cutting.

MAKES ENOUGH TO COVER ONE 23 CM CAKE

CHOCOLATE FROSTING

6 tablespoons Cadbury Bournville Cocoa, sifted

3 cups (500 g) icing sugar, sifted

1½ tablespoons liquid glucose

75 g unsalted butter, softened

2½ tablespoons water

1 Slowly blend the sifted cocoa and icing sugar, glucose syrup and butter in a mixing bowl.

2 When combined, slowly add the water, beating all the time.

3 When the ingredients have again been combined beat the mixture for a further 15 minutes until the frosting is light and fluffy.

MAKES ENOUGH TO COVER ONE 23 CM CAKE

❖ **FROSTINGS**

A frosting is a sweet icing which should form a slightly hard, thin crust on the outside and be soft on the inside.

To store: always keep frosting covered with a damp cloth or store in an airtight container

CHOC-TAILS

Not only can you have chocolate for breakfast, lunch and dinner but you can also relax and enjoy the ultimate in liquid sustenance.

The Step-by-Step Technique for this chapter shows the making of *The Ultimate Hot Chocolate*.

The Ultimate Hot Chocolate

STEP-BY-STEP TECHNIQUES

THE ULTIMATE HOT CHOCOLATE

6 Pascal's marshmallows

1 cup (250 ml) milk, brought to the boil

1 teaspoon Cadbury Bournville Cocoa

1 teaspoon Cadbury Drinking Chocolate

1 tablespoon cognac

extra cocoa for dusting

1 Place three of the marshmallows into the hot milk and stir until they have melted.

2 Pour half of the boiled milk over the cocoa and drinking chocolate and stir until they are dissolved.

3 Add the cognac to the chocolate milk and pour in the other half of the milk mixture.

4 Pour into a mug and set the other marshmallows on top of the drink and quickly dust with a little cocoa.

5 Drink while still hot.

SERVES 1 TO 2

Place three marshmallows into hot, boiled milk and stir until melted.

Pour half of milk over the cocoa and drinking chocolate and stir until dissolved.

Add cognac to the chocolate milk and then add the rest of the milk.

CHOCOLATE FROG NOG

2 x Cadbury Strawberry Freddo Frogs

1 cup (250 ml) milk, brought to the boil

1 tablespoon Cadbury Drinking Chocolate

3 tablespoons whipped cream

extra drinking chocolate for dusting

1 Place the Strawberry Freddo Frogs into the hot milk and stir until they are melted and mixed with the liquid.

2 Add the liquid slowly to the drinking chocolate and stir to dissolve.

3 Spoon the whipped cream over the top of the drink and dust lightly with extra drinking chocolate.

SERVES 1

MALLOW MILKSHAKE

1 cup (250 ml) milk

4 Pascal's marshmallows

1 tablespoon brown sugar

2 tablespoons finely grated Cadbury Dark Cooking Chocolate

3 teaspoons Cadbury Drinking Chocolate, for dusting

1 Place all ingredients into a blender and blend on highest setting for 3 minutes.

2 Pour into a tumbler and dust lightly with Cadbury Drinking Chocolate.

SERVES 1

CHOC CHOC CHOC-TAIL

3 tablespoons Crème de Cacao

1 tablespoon Cadbury Drinking Chocolate

2 to 3 ice cubes

¾ cup (200 ml) thickened cream

2 tablespoons Cadbury Dark Cooking Chocolate, grated

1 tablespoon Cadbury Dark Cooking Chocolate, grated, for decoration

1 Place all ingredients into an electric blender and blend on high speed for 1 minute.

2 Pour into a cold cocktail glass and sprinkle the top of the drink with dark chocolate shavings.

SERVES 1 TO 2

STRAW STOPPER

2 tablespoons strawberry or plain yoghurt

1 tablespoon Cadbury Drinking Chocolate

4 to 5 whole fresh strawberries, washed and hulled

1 cup (250 ml) fresh milk

1 tablespoon Cadbury Chocolate Dots

Cadbury Drinking Chocolate for dusting

1 Place all ingredients into an electric blender and blend on high speed for 1 minute.

2 Pour liquid into a chilled glass and dust lightly with Cadbury Drinking Chocolate.

SERVES 1

LIQUEUR LIPSMACKER

2½ tablespoons Cointreau

1 tablespoon fresh lemon juice

1 tablespoon fresh orange juice

2 tablespoons Cadbury White Cooking Chocolate, finely grated

2 to 3 ice cubes

Strawberrries dipped in white chocolate, to serve

1 Place all ingredients into an electric blender and blend on high setting for 1 minute.

2 Pour liquid into a chilled cocktail glass.

3 Serve with strawberries dipped in white chocolate.

SERVES 1

On following pages, from left to right:
Mallow Milkshake,
Straw Stopper, Choc Choc
Choc-Tail, Liqueur
Lipsmacker

QUESTIONS & ANSWERS

Where should I store chocolates?

Chocolate should be well wrapped and stored in a cool dry place
- not the fridge.

What is the best way to melt chocolate?

Instructions are given on the pack for melting. Always
remember chocolate is to be melted not cooked. Too high a
temperature or for too long will cause the chocolate to 'sieze'
into hard grainy lumps. Melt chocolate over a double boiler or a
bowl over simmering water taking care no water drips into the
chocolate. Never melt chocolate over direct heat as it is too hot
and will burn the chocolate. Chocolate melts very successfully
in the microwave oven.

Why does my chocolate go blotchy on setting?

Chocolate will 'bloom' or form a greyish-white appearance on
the surface if the chocolate has been exposed to severe
temperature changes i.e. being stored in too cold a temperature
(refrigerated) or too hot a temperature. It affects the appearance
but not the flavour and doesn't mean the chocolate is 'off'.

Can I add liquids to chocolate?

Small amounts of fluid can spoil chocolate. A drop of water
added to melted chocolate will cause it to thicken and spoil.
Nothing can be done to rectify the problem. Chocolate can be
safely melted with a small amount of liquid such as cream or
alcohol if they are put in the bowl together then heated.
Chocolate can be placed into a hot liquid and allowed to melt
away from the heat, stirring it into the liquid.

What do I do when my chocolate gets too thick?

Chocolate will slowly thicken on setting., it can be successfully
remelted to a liquid form again. If the chocolate has overheated
it may become too thick. The addition of oil or copha may help
to liquify the chocolate.

How do I stop my chocolate curls breaking?

When using a grater to make chocolate curls the chocolate
should be at a warm room temperature. If the chocolate is too
cold it will break rather than form long dark curls. Chocolate
can be warmed in the microwave oven on a low setting but do
not allow it to melt.

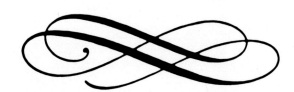

PRODUCT GLOSSARY

Cadbury, Australia has an extensive range of both Cadbury pure chocolate products and Unichoc compounded chocolate products. They are:

- Cadbury Dark Cooking Chocolate 250 g
- Cadbury Milk Cooking Chocolate 250 g
- Cadbury White Cooking Chocolate 250 g
- Cadbury Chocolate Dots 200 g
- Cadbury Bournville Cocoa 125 g
- Cadbury Bournville Cocoa 250 g
- Cadbury Bournville Cocoa 375 g
- Cadbury Drinking Chocolate 250 g
- Cadbury Drinking Chocolate 500 g
- Unichoc Dark Buttons 375 g
- Unichoc MilkButtons 375 g
- Unichoc WhiteButtons 375 g
- Unichoc Dark Compounded Block 300 g
- Unichoc Milk Compounded Block 300 g

Cadbury New Zealand range consists of:

- Cadbury Cooking Chocolate 150 g - A pure, dark chocolate product which is specially designed for successful baking.
- Cadbury Bournville Cocoa 250 g - as Australian product.
- Cadbury Chocolate Chips - 250 g and 400 g - pure, dark chocolate cylindrical chips which are suitable for baking. Can be used for sauces and topping as well as biscuit or slice baking and decorating cakes and desserts.
- Cadbury Chocolate Dots 200 g - as Australian product.

MEASURING MADE EASY

HOW TO MEASURE LIQUIDS

METRIC	IMPERIAL	CUPS
30 ml	1 fluid ounce	1 tablespoon plus 2 teaspoons
60 ml	2 fluid ounces	¼ cup
90 ml	3 fluid ounces	
125 ml	4 fluid ounces	½ cup
150 ml	5 fluid ounces	
170 ml	5½ fluid ounces	
180 ml	6 fluid ounces	¾ cup
220 ml	7 fluid ounces	
250 ml	8 fluid ounces	1 cup
500 ml	16 fluid ounces	2 cups
600 ml	20 fluid ounces (1 pint)	2½ cups
1 litre	1¾ pints	

HOW TO MEASURE DRY INGREDIENTS

15 g	½ oz	
30 g	1 oz	
60 g	2 oz	
90 g	3 oz	
125 g	4 oz	(¼ lb)
155 g	5 oz	
185 g	6 oz	
220 g	7 oz	
250 g	8 oz	(½ lb)
280 g	9 oz	
315 g	10 oz	
345 g	11 oz	
375 g	12 oz	(¾ lb)
410 g	13 oz	
440 g	14 oz	
470 g	15 oz	
500 g	16 oz	(1 lb)
750 g	24 oz	(1½ lb)
1 kg	32 oz	(2 lb)

QUICK CONVERSIONS

5 mm	¼ inch	
1 cm	½ inch	
2 cm	¾ inch	
2.5 cm	1 inch	
5 cm	2 inches	
6 cm	2½ inches	
8 cm	3 inches	
10 cm	4 inches	
12 cm	5 inches	
15 cm	6 inches	
18 cm	7 inches	
20 cm	8 inches	
23 cm	9 inches	
25 cm	10 inches	
28 cm	11 inches	
30 cm	12 inches	(1 foot)
46 cm	18 inches	
50 cm	20 inches	
61 cm	24 inches	(2 feet)
77 cm	30 inches	

NOTE: We developed the recipes in this book in Australia where the tablespoon measure is 20 ml. In many other countries the tablespoon is 15 ml. For most recipes this difference will not be noticeable.

However, for recipes using baking powder, gelatine, bicarbonate of soda, small amounts of flour and cornflour, we suggest you add an extra teaspoon for each tablespoon specified

USING CUPS AND SPOONS

All cup and spoon measurements are level

METRIC CUP				METRIC SPOONS	
¼ cup	60 ml	2 fluid ounces		¼ teaspoon	1¼ ml
⅓ cup	80 ml	2½ fluid ounces		½ teaspoon	2½ ml
½ cup	125 ml	4 fluid ounces		1 teaspoon	5 ml
1 cup	250 ml	8 fluid ounces		1 tablespoon	20 ml

OVEN TEMPERATURES

TEMPERATURES	CELSIUS (°C)	FAHRENHEIT (°F)	GAS MARK
Very slow	120	250	½
Slow	150	300	2
Moderately slow	160-180	325-350	3-4
Moderate	190-200	375-400	5-6
Moderately hot	220-230	425-450	7
Hot	250-260	475-500	8-9

INDEX